# Women, Work, and Family

# Women, Work, and Family

## Dimensions of Change in American Society

Frank L. Mott

with

Steven H. Sandell
David Shapiro
Patricia K. Brito
Timothy J. Carr
Carol Jusenius
Peter J. Koenig
Sylvia F. Moore

Center for Human Resource Research
The Ohio State University

**Lexington Books**
D.C. Heath and Company
Lexington, Massachusetts
Toronto

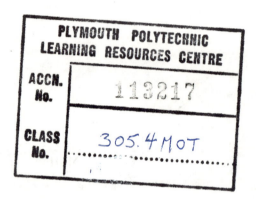
*Copyright © 1978 by D.C. Heath and Company.*

Published simultaneously in Canada.

Printed in the United States of America.

International Standard Book Number: 0-669-02092-3

Library of Congress Catalog Card Number: 77-18329

# Contents

# List of Figures

# List of Tables

# Preface

For more than a decade the Center for Human Resource Research of The Ohio State University and the U.S. Bureau of the Census, under separate contracts with the Employment and Training Administration of the U.S. Department of Labor, have been engaged in the National Longitudinal Surveys (NLS) of labor market experience. Four subsets of the United States civilian population are being studied: young men who at the inception of the study were fourteen to twenty-four years of age; a counterpart group of young women; women thirty to forty-four years of age; and men forty-five to fifty-nine years of age. These groups were selected because each is confronted with special labor market problems that are challenging to policymakers: for the middle-aged men, problems of skill obsolescence and deteriorating health that may make reemployment difficult if jobs are lost; for the older group of women, problems associated with reentry to the labor market after children are in school or grown; and for the young men and women, the problems revolving around occupational choice, preparation for work, and the often difficult period of accommodation to the labor market when formal schooling has been completed.

For each of these four population groups a national probability sample of the noninstitutional civilian population was drawn by the Census Bureau in 1966. Interviews have been conducted periodically by census enumerators using questionnaires prepared by the Center for Human Resource Research. Originally contemplated as covering a five-year period, the surveys have been so successful and attrition so small that they have been continued beyond the initially planned expiration dates. As of the middle of 1978, interviews with all four cohorts are continuing. It is contemplated that all four groups will be interviewed for at least fifteen years. In addition, interviews with two new cohorts of youth will begin in early 1979 under the auspices of the U.S. Department of Labor, with the interviews being conducted by the National Opinion Research Center, Chicago, Illinois.

While accepting sole responsibility for whatever limitations the volume may have, we wish to acknowledge our debt to the many people who helped us in preparing this volume. These include Howard Rosen, the Director of the Office of Research and Development of the U.S. Department of Labors' Employment and Training Administration; and Ellen Sehgal, who has for several years been the monitor for this project.

The research staff of the Center for Human Resource Research has enjoyed the continuous expert and friendly collaboration of personnel of the Bureau of the Census, who have been responsible for developing the samples, conducting all of the interviews, coding and editing the data, and preparing the initial versions of the computer tapes.

The programming required for the analyses in this volume was the responsibility of the Data Processing Unit of the Center for Human Resource Research under the direction of Carol Sheets. Especial thanks go to Rufus Milsted, Tom Steedman, Ron Taylor, and Pete Tomasek, whose programming and other technical assistance were of invaluable assistance to us in preparing this report.

Herbert S. Parnes provided us with his continuing guidance and advice. We also owe debts of gratitude to our colleagues Stan Benecki, Steven Hills, Gilbert Nestel, and Lois Shaw of the Center, who generously provided of their time in carefully reviewing the various drafts of this volume. In addition, thanks go out to our former colleagues John T. Grasso, Andrew I. Kohen, and Richard Shortlidge, who provided helpful comments. In addition to the research assistance mentioned in the specific chapters, we would particularly like to acknowledge the work of R. Jean Haurin and Ellen Mumma, who, over a period of many months, carried out the thankless task of coordinating, fact checking, proofreading, and editing this volume.

Finally, the authors are especially indebted to Jeanie Barnes, who impeccably typed endless versions of this report, always with a tight deadline, and always with a smile. Her ability to translate unreadable scribbles into the English language was nothing short of miraculous. For her skillful assistance we are most grateful.

*Frank L. Mott* March 1978

# Women, Work, and
# Family

# 1 Introduction and Overview

*Frank L. Mott*

In recent years, the popular and academic literature has focused extensively on issues connected with the women's liberation movement. There have been extensive treatments focusing on issues concerning women's changing attitudes regarding their home and work roles as well as changes in their behavior—encompassing work activity, marital and family behavior patterns, and the myriad of activities associated with their work, career, and family roles. As is often the case with issues of major social and political import, ideas, value judgments and popular impressions tend to be more extensively available than facts on which rational decisions can be based. This book represents one small step toward providing necessary hard evidence.

Young American women who were fourteen to twenty-four years of age in 1968—the focus of this study—represent the "cutting edge" of this process of change in American society. We will follow these women over the 1968 to 1973 period and examine changes in their attitudes and behaviors along a number of important dimensions—education, marriage, family, job, and career. To the extent that these young women do indeed represent the "new wave" of American womanhood, this study, which focuses on a representative national sample of young adults, provides important new evidence that occasionally supports and sometimes is inconsistent with popular ideas and notions.

Admittedly, the 1968 to 1973 period is now, to some extent, history. However, it is an extremely important period of our history since it encompassed major political, economic, and social transitions. At the same time, economic and social trends that developed during the period have, for the most part, continued unabated. Most importantly, what we focus on in this volume are the interactions between socioeconomic backgrounds, educational development, family events, and work. There is considerable evidence that the nature of these interactions continues relatively unchanged. As such, the women who were studied in this volume are probably representative of the current generation of young women reaching adulthood.

These studies are part of a larger, even more comprehensive research project that the Center for Human Resource Research, under the sponsorship of the U.S. Department of Labor, is undertaking. As such, many of the materials included are only partial representations and, in essence, summaries of more extensive studies. The interested reader is invited to contact the Center if he or she wishes further elaboration on a given theme. Space constraints have limited our ability to include all related materials. Thus we have endeavored to

1

concentrate on those dimensions most related to our major theme—social change in American society.

## Plan of the Volume

The chapters in this volume focus on various dimensions of the theme elaborated earlier. Most of this chapter provides an overview of the socioeconomic changes for young women who were fourteen to twenty-four years of age in 1968. These are ages when most young women complete their schooling, form permanent relationships and, in many instances, become mothers and enter the job market for the first time. This chapter focuses on changes associated with the aging process as well as on trends in work and family attitudes and behavior patterns associated with secular changes over the period. As is seen later, some of the secular trends highlighted here are of fundamental importance for explaining the behavior patterns indicated in many of the remaining chapters.

Chapter 2 examines an important aspect of the preparation for the world of work—college attendance. More specifically, it investigates the factors associated with desires and expectations for higher education, as well as factors related to actual college attendance. These are important topics since they have profound implications for the future labor market behavior and family experiences of young women. One unique aspect of this chapter relates to the examination of the college attendance patterns of young black women. While the association between background factors and the likelihood of college attendance have been generally established, the black pattern of association is less well known. Chapter 2 presents some surprising results with regard to the college desires and expectations of black young women—after one has taken into account racial differences in socioeconomic background.

Chapter 3 focuses on the labor force dynamics associated with withdrawal from and reentry into the labor force when a woman bears her first child. This chapter studies in great detail a point in the life cycle that has heretofore been examined only superficially, and suggests several socioeconomic rationales for the differences between white and black behavior patterns. It also provides dramatic evidence of the strong and increasing labor force attachment of many young mothers.

While it is known that many young women do leave the work force for the duration of time when they have their first child, what is not generally known is that large proportions of women, particularly black women, very quickly return to work. The "success" women of different races and socioeconomic statuses have in regaining meaningful employment is considered in some detail.

Shifting somewhat from current to prospective labor force activities, chapter 4 examines the characteristics of young women that are associated with the choice of an "atypical" occupation or one traditionally considered to be a "male" job. Considering the increasing proportion of young women planning careers and the presumed importance of the women's liberation movement, this chapter includes some rather surprising results regarding the kinds of jobs most women propose to enter. The chapter relates these prospective occupational plans to the anticipated demands of the American labor market and, from a policy perspective, reaches some important conclusions.

Also employing the longer time span, chapter 5 addresses the question of whether investment in on-the-job training is related to an expectation of long-term attachment to the labor force. That is, are women who anticipate extensive lifetime labor force attachment more likely than their less committed counterparts to take jobs with larger training components and lower initial wages? Thus the theme of "economically rational" behavior wends its way through several chapters. Given the apparent increasing tendency for women to be seeking careers, are they making rational choices from the perspective of choosing career lines that (1) have a future and, (2) pay well and, if so, are they properly preparing themselves for these occupations?

Chapter 6 analyzes some of the causes as well as the consequences of migration for the economic welfare of young women and their families. Focusing on married family units, are the work activities of the wife being fully considered from both an economic and noneconomic perspective when the family considers making a move? Since about one-third of the young women were living in a different county or metropolitan area in 1973 than in 1968, this topic is important.

Marital disruption is another phenomenon that affects the lives of surprisingly large numbers of young women. About 12 percent of the white women and more than 30 percent of the black women who were married at any time between 1968 and 1973 experienced a separation or divorce during that five-year period. Chapter 7 examines some of the determinants of marital disruption and also analyzes in some detail the short-run economic consequences for women and their children. The longitudinal nature of the data make them ideal for this kind of analysis, for one can follow the same young women from an intact marriage, through the disruption transition process, and into the early phases of postdisruption life.

## The National Longitudinal Surveys of Young Women

### The Sample

In early 1968, the U.S. Bureau of the Census, under contract with the Employment and Training Administration of the U.S. Department of Labor, interviewed a nationally representative cross section of 5,159 young women aged fourteen to twenty-four, including 3,638 white and 1,459 black respondents.[1]

Black women were deliberately oversampled to provide a sufficiently large number of blacks for statistically reliable racial comparisons.[2] These women were reinterviewed each year through 1973. The interviews included extensive batteries of questions relating to their education, employment, family life, and a host of other characteristics that were hypothesized to affect or reflect labor market experience.

As of the 1973 survey, fully 4,424 of the original 5,159 respondents were still being interviewed, representing 85.8 percent of the original sample—86.5 percent of the whites and 84.3 percent of the blacks. Thus, reflecting the diligent field work of the Bureau of the Census, attrition from the sample has been relatively low and no major nonresponse biases are known to exist.

Reflecting the sampling procedures used by the Bureau of the Census, the separate black and white samples as well as the combined race sample must be appropriately weighted to provide accurate population estimates. For this reason, unless otherwise specified, all of the tabular and multivariate analyses in this volume are based on weighted data. However, in all of the tabular and multivariate material the term "number of respondents" refers to the unweighted number of young women in the sample studied.

*Nature of the Data*

The uniqueness of the National Longitudinal Surveys (NLS) rests in the panel nature of the data—that is, information is provided at a number of points in time for the same group of respondents. Thus it is possible to examine in some detail the dynamics of a young woman's activities. For example, from an employment perspective, one can follow a woman job by job through the 1968 to 1973 period. One can also view changes in her educational activities and in her family and household status. Obviously, all of these and other behavior patterns can be juxtaposed, depending on one's research interests, with a view to ascertaining the relationships that exist both at a given time and over time. In this context, the longitudinal character of the data permits one to go much further in establishing directions of causation than is possible with cross-sectional data. For example, that attitudes or psychological orientations measured at one point in time are related to subsequent behavior increases the likelihood that the attitude is conditioning rather than merely reflecting the behavior.

A number of chapters in this volume take advantage of this unique longitudinal dimension of the data set. The chapter on college attendance follows young women from their final high-school year through the early posthigh-school years, comparing the likelihood of college attendance for women with different background characteristics. The following chapter, which focuses on work activity surrounding the first birth event, examines the ability of women to attain their prebirth wage in their first postbirth job; an analysis that is possible only with a data set that follows the same women over a period of time. Chapter 4 suggests how—even during the brief 1968 to 1973 time period—there were significant transitions in the kinds of careers young women plan to pursue in the years ahead.

Chapter 6, which examines the socioeconomic determinants and consequences of geographic mobility, also utilizes longitudinal aspects of the data set by comparing locational characteristics of the same women at different points in time, examining, in particular, income- and work-related characteristics of the respondents before and after the moves. Without the temporal dimensions of the data set, much of this analysis would not be possible. Finally, the NLS data make it possible to examine in great detail socioeconomic determinants and consequences of the marital disruption process. Thus most of the analyses in this volume are heavily contingent on the availability of panel data and, as such, could not have been accomplished so successfully with standard cross-sectional data and methodological procedures.

## 1968 to 1973: A Descriptive Overview

For a substantial portion of the cohort of young women under consideration in this volume, the years between 1968 and 1973 represent a period of maturation. The youngest five-year age group, all of whom were in their teens when the study began, were nineteen to twenty-three in 1973. Thus, for many of these women, the five-year interval encompassed leaving school, labor market entry, marriage or the forming of other permanent relationships, and childbearing.

In addition to this maturational process, the 1968 to 1973 period is often felt to be a period of significant social change that might be evidenced by changes in family formation patterns, work behavior, and attitudes for women of a given age. For this reason, in addition to highlighting overall trends for the entire NLS young women's cohort over the half decade, separate comparisons are made, where appropriate, between women who were twenty to twenty-four in 1968 and those of the same ages in 1973.

### Changes in Household and Family Status

Figure 1-1 highlights in a summary manner many of the maturational patterns of change. The proportion of the cohort enrolled in school declined from 52.1 to 13.4 percent for the white young women, and from 48.2 to 13.3 percent for their black counterparts.[3] Paralleling this decline, there were major shifts in household and marital patterns, as evidenced by the sharp decline in the proportions of young women living with their parents and the concomitant increase in the percentages who were married. There are significant racial

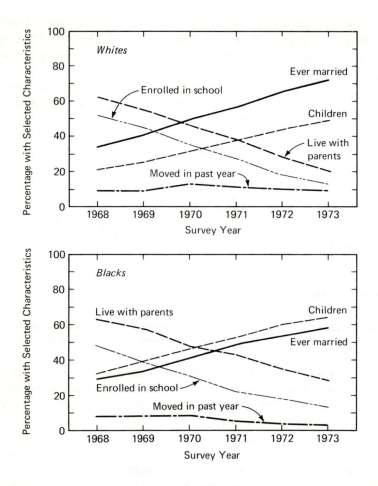

**Figure 1-1.** Trends in Selected Sociodemographic Characteristics for White and Black Women, 1968 to 1973

variations in some of these changes. Whereas in 1968 the household compositions and marital statuses of the young black and white women are somewhat similar, by 1973 there are dramatic distinctions. In 1973, 42 percent of the black women had never been married and 17 percent were either separated, divorced or widowed, compared with only 27 and 6 percent, respectively, for the white women. Although two-thirds of the white women were in an intact marriage, only two-fifths of the black women were living with husbands. Parallel differences between blacks and whites are evident in the data on household status. Black women in 1973 are somewhat more likely than white women to be living with their parents and are twice as likely to be in a living arrangement that does not include either parents or a husband. These data suggest that, from the perspective of living arrangements, the transition to adulthood for the average black woman may be far more complex than for her white counterpart. They also suggest that substantially greater proportions of young adult black women need employment as a primary means of supporting themselves during this difficult transition period.

While a comparison of statuses at just two points in time five years apart is an obvious simplification of the dynamics of change, there is one other major point worth noting. Whereas black women were less likely to move into a marriage during the half decade, they were much more likely to move out of marriage. About one-tenth of the white women who were married in 1968 were either separated, widowed or divorced in 1973, compared with one-third of their black counterparts. This large and growing group requires special employment-related assistance, a fact highlighted in chapter 7.

These cohort trends in changes in family and marital status represent more than just an aging process. Comparing black and white young women who were twenty to twenty-four years of age in 1968 with women the same age in 1973, certain secular trends may be noted. There appears to be a trend toward delayed marriages, as indicated by higher proportions never married in 1973 and lower proportions married and living with their husbands. Also, the proportion of women aged twenty to twenty-four who were separated or divorced increased over the five-year period. All of these changes are consistent with the significantly greater proportions of white and black women living in "other" household relationships—not with parents or a husband. Indeed, as may be noted in table 1-1, by 1973, about 19 percent of white and fully a third of black twenty- to twenty-four-year-old women were not living with either their parents or their spouse. On the average, these women presumably may have a greater need for self-earned income than would women living in other household arrangements.

Paralleling these rather dramatic changes in household and marital status are sharp increases in the percentage of women with children. The percentage of white women who have had at least one child increases from slightly under one-fourth to about one-half during the five-year period, and the corresponding proportion for black women increases from one-third to about two-thirds. Indeed, the childbearing period for these women is far from complete—consistent with the knowledge that the youngest women in the study are only nineteen years of age as of 1973. Over 60 percent of the white and 50 percent of the black women who had no children in 1968 still had not given birth by 1973.

It is useful to consider further the demographic transition process these women are currently undergoing. Only about 6 percent of those white women who were fifteen to nineteen in 1968 had borne a child as of that date. By 1973, about 36 percent of this group had borne at least one child. Shifting momen-

**Table 1-1**

**Household Structure for Selected Age Groups in 1968 and 1973 by Race [a]**

*(Percentage Distributions)*

| Household Structure | 1968 | | 1973 | |
|---|---|---|---|---|
| | *Age 15-19* | *Age 20-24* | *Age 20-24* | *Age 25-29* |
| | | *Whites* | | |
| Number of respondents | 1,571 | 1,301 | 1,571 | 1,301 |
| Total percent | 100.0 | 100.0 | 100.0 | 100.0 |
| Lived with parents[b] | 86.0 | 28.9 | 26.9 | 7.0 |
| Lived with husband | 9.0 | 58.1 | 54.3 | 80.2 |
| Other | 4.9 | 13.0 | 18.7 | 12.8 |
| | | *Blacks* | | |
| Number of respondents | 686 | 426 | 686 | 426 |
| Total percent | 100.0 | 100.0 | 100.0 | 100.0 |
| Lived with parents[b] | 80.9 | 34.9 | 33.7 | 16.2 |
| Lived with husband | 7.7 | 41.0 | 32.9 | 51.2 |
| Other | 11.4 | 24.1 | 33.5 | 32.6 |

[a]Universe consists of respondents who were interviewed in 1968 and 1973.

[b]Includes very small percentages of respondents living with parents and husband.

tarily from one age group to another, between 1968 and 1973, the proportion of women who were mothers among those who were twenty to twenty-four in *1968* increased from about 43 to 71 percent.

Whereas the preceding characteristics represent the increase in motherhood due to aging per se, a not surprising phenomenon, the secular change for a given age group over the five-year period is actually in the opposite direction. As may be noted in table 1-2, among white women the proportion of twenty- to twenty-four-year olds without children increased fairly sharply from 57 to 64 percent—consistent with the marriage and household information noted earlier. This trend toward childlessness or a later average age for childbearing has major implications for the proportion of young adult women who can be expected to seek employment now and in the years ahead.

While the longitudinal dimensions of the NLS do not permit measuring secular changes in the fertility patterns of women aged twenty-five to twenty-nine in 1973, there is one important point worth noting concerning this group. Since the average black woman in the original fourteen- to twenty-four-year-old cohort began her childbearing at a somewhat earlier age, she is now further along in her family building process than is her white counterpart—that is, an examination of the distribution of twenty-five- to twenty-nine-year-old black and white women by parent status indicates that even though a slightly higher proportion of the black women have borne a child by 1973, a significantly

**Table 1-2**

**Percentage Distribution and Labor Force Participation Rate in 1968 and 1973 by Parental Status and Race for Twenty to Twenty-four Year Olds[a]**

| | 1968 | | 1973 | |
|---|---|---|---|---|
| Parental Status | Percentage Distribution | Labor Force Participation Rate | Percentage Distribution | Labor Force Participation Rate |
| | Whites | | | |
| Number of respondents | 1,301 | 1,290 | 1,570 | 1,564 |
| Total | 100.0 | 57.8 | 100.0 | 65.7 |
| No own children present | 57.4 | 75.5 | 64.2 | 77.0 |
| Own children present | 42.5 | 34.4 | 35.8 | 41.1 |
| | Blacks | | | |
| Number of respondents | 425 | 419 | 686 | 679 |
| Total | 100.0 | 60.5 | 100.0 | 62.8 |
| No own children present | 42.8 | 73.7 | 41.6 | 71.2 |
| Own children present | 57.2 | 51.4 | 58.4 | 57.2 |

[a]Universe consists of respondents who were interviewed in 1968 and 1973.

higher proportion of those with children now have a youngest child of school age (about 31 percent for black twenty-five- to twenty-nine-year-old women, compared with only 22 percent for the white women). This evidence strongly supports the notion (documented in some detail in chapter 3) that this generation of black women intend to have only a limited number of children and either are or soon will be seeking meaningful employment opportunities for a lifetime of work.

*Changes in Labor Force Participation*

The association between childbearing and employment status may be noted from the overall labor force participation rates and the percentages of women with children described in figures 1-1 and 1-2. The impact of the birth event and of changes in child status can, however, be specified more directly. Women who were without children both in 1968 and 1973 had by far the sharpest increases in labor force participation during the period. In 1968 their rates were only moderate, reflecting their younger average age and greater school enrollment rates. By 1973, the majority of these women had entered employment. White labor force participation rates for this group increased from 46 to 78 percent between 1968 and 1973, and the black rate increased from 37 to 71 percent. In all likelihood, many individuals in this group will show significant but temporary

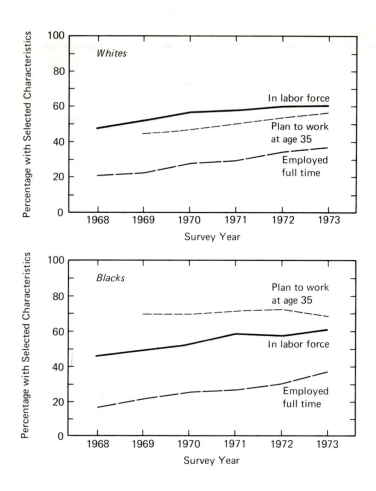

**Figure 1-2.** Trends in Selected Socioeconomic Characteristics for White and Black Women, 1968 to 1973

declines in their labor force participation in the immediate years ahead as they enter their childbearing years. In contrast, white women who had their first child between 1968 and 1973 evidenced sharp declines in participation, whereas black women in this category evidenced a modest increase in participation. Even though each of these women had a child of preschool age in the home, about 42 percent of the white women and 57 percent of the black were in the labor force at the time of their 1973 interview. This group is analyzed in detail in chapter 3.

Finally, women who had their first child before 1968 had minor increases in participation during the period, partly reflecting the aging of their youngest child. White labor force participation rates for this group increased about 9 percentage points, compared with a more modest increase of 3 percentage points for the blacks.

The longitudinal character of the data set may be used to probe somewhat further into the dynamics of this labor force transition. For example, while the labor force participation rate for all white women in the sample increased by about 13 percentage points between the 1968 and 1973 interview dates, in actuality about 16 percent of the women were in the labor force in 1968 and out in 1973. Conversely, 29 percent were out in 1968 but had entered by 1973. For the black women, labor force participation increased by 16 percentage points, representing a "netting out" of the 30 percent who entered the labor force and the 14 percent who exited. These estimates are, of course, gross understatements of the actual flows into and out of the labor force during the period, as a given individual could well have had numerous such moves during the five-year period.

These patterns are useful for describing the general nature of the association between work and childbearing. They also demonstrate that whenever one generalizes about such patterns for a group as diverse as a full cross section of young women, one must be aware that there are substantial numbers of individuals whose experiences run counter to the described pattern. It may well be that these divergent groups, from program and policy perspectives, represent individuals with special and different needs. For example, it is not unreasonable to speculate that the 15 percent of all white women and 27 percent of all black women who gave birth to a first child between 1968 and 1973 and entered the labor force during that period represent women with a very high commitment or strong economic need to work. As such, they may well be especially worthy of careful analysis.

Much of the preceding discussion has highlighted secular changes and changes in both demographic and labor force characteristics of young women associated with the maturation process. The overall labor force participation changes cited largely reflect changes in household and family structure. Focusing once again, somewhat more narrowly, on the twenty- to twenty-four-year-old groups in 1968 and 1973, some rather dramatic short-term secular changes may be noted. The overall labor force participation rate for white twenty- to twenty-four-year olds increased from about 58 to 66 percent in the short five-year period (table 1-2). Note that this secular change does *not* reflect a demographic phenomenon, but rather a dramatic 11 percentage point increase in the participation rate between the survey dates of twenty- to twenty-four-year-old women with children. A smaller, but still notable trend was evidenced for black women. Thus, independent of all the demographic factors noted earlier, there have been major changes in the willingness and desire of young women with children to participate in the labor force.

Several secular trends have been documented or at least alluded to here.

They include apparent changes in patterns of household and family relation-ships, changes in childbearing patterns, as well as secular increases in working propensities. All of these factors undoubtedly represent components of the generally acknowledged movement toward greater equality between the sexes in the rights and responsibilities of adulthood.

### Changes in Other Work-related Characteristics

Not only was there a significant net movement into the labor force between 1968 and 1973, but for those women working in these two years there is some evidence of occupational upgrading during that period. The proportion of employed white women in professional jobs increased from about 15 to 22 percent. For black women, the increase was from about 6 to 12 percent. For both white and black women, there were increases in other white-collar employment, and significant declines in employment in service occupations. For whites, much of the occupational upgrading reflected the movement out of school by women who were employed in both 1968 and 1973, as evidenced by significant increases in professional and other white-collar employment for fifteen- to nineteen-year olds between 1968 and 1973 but only marginal increases for twenty- to twenty-four-year olds. For blacks, occupational up-grading was more evenly divided between women who were aged fifteen to nineteen in 1968 and women who were twenty to twenty-four, reflecting at least in part the more delayed entry of blacks into the nonstudent labor force.

Coincident with the occupational upgrading were increases in real hourly wages (in 1967 dollars) for women of both races who were working in both years. For whites, the increase was from $1.55 to $2.22, or 43 percent. For blacks, average hourly earnings rose from $1.48 to $1.95, an increase of 32 percent. Thus there is evidence of increased earnings over time associated with increased work experience and, perhaps, with maturation per se. This issue is considered in some detail in chapter 5.[4]

### Some Perspectives on Attitude Changes

There is very little evidence of unhappiness with work among those women in our sample with the most extensive work attachment. Focusing on those women employed in 1968 and 1973, fully 90 percent of the white and 85 percent of the black women said they liked their 1968 jobs. There were only minor changes in these feelings between 1968 and 1973, since the decline in the proportion who liked their jobs "very much" (about 10 percentage points) was offset by a corresponding rise in the proportion who liked their job "somewhat." Also at the disaggregated level, whereas fewer than 10 percent of those who liked their jobs in 1968 disliked their jobs in 1973, more than 80 percent of those who had disliked their jobs in 1968 liked them in 1973. (There was no difference in responses of fifteen- to nineteen-year olds in 1968 and twenty- to twenty-four-year olds in this regard.) There are several possible explanations for this. First, unhappy workers are probably more likely to leave the labor force if they have the option to do so. Second, unhappy workers undoubtedly are more likely to change jobs in a search for more satisfactory working conditions.

In addition to the specific feelings of job satisfaction of the working group of women, there is evidence of a profound change between 1968 and 1972 in the attitudes of young women toward the propriety of labor market activity on the part of mothers of young children.[5] One might anticipate some shift toward more positive attitudes about work among young women as they mature, marry, and gain work experience. However, of greatest interest is the question of whether there are secular forces at work that have caused women with the same characteristics to be more positively disposed toward work outside the home. Table 1-3 provides some dramatic evidence in this regard. Within a given year (either 1968 or 1972), there is only weak evidence of shifts toward more positive work attitudes as one moves from younger to older respondents. However, if one compares eighteen- to twenty-one- or twenty-one- to twenty-four-year olds *across* years, there are large shifts toward more positive attitudes. For example, the proportion who believe that it is acceptable for a young

**Table 1-3**

**Percentage of Women with Positive Reactions to Work Role for Women in 1968 and 1972 by Age and Conditions of Work[a]**

| | Percent with Positive Response | |
|---|---|---|
| Age and Work Conditions | 1968 | 1972 |
| 18 to 21 years | | |
| Number of respondents | 1,766 | 1,799 |
| All right to work if: | | |
| (1) economic necessity | 91.2 | 93.6 |
| (2) husband and wife agree | 65.5 | 80.0 |
| (3) even if husband disagrees | 12.0 | 24.3 |
| 21 to 24 years | | |
| Number of respondents | 1,362 | 1,839 |
| All right to work if: | | |
| (1) economic necessity | 90.7 | 94.6 |
| (2) husband and wife agree | 66.7 | 83.4 |
| (3) even if husband disagrees | 12.6 | 26.6 |

[a]Universe consists of respondents who were interviewed in 1968 and 1972. For descriptions of questions, see footnote 5 of this chapter.

mother to work if the husband and wife agree increases from 66 to 80 percent for eighteen- to twenty-one-year olds and from 67 to 83 percent for twenty-one to twenty-four-year olds in the four-year period. Large increases also occur in the item asking if it is acceptable to work even if the husband disagrees.

Focusing more narrowly on the responses of ever-married women, one finds the same trends. When the question is whether labor market activity by the mother of young children is appropriate if her husband agrees, the proportions of positive responses among (the same) white women increased sharply from about 68 to 85 percent over the four-year period. The same pattern was found when married fifteen- to nineteen- and twenty- to twenty-four-year olds were examined separately. Less dramatic increases occurred for black women, reflecting the higher level of positive responses by these women in 1968. It is also of some interest to note that whereas only 12 percent of the white women who gave a positive response in 1968 had shifted to a negative response by 1972, fully 79 percent of those who had a negative attitude in 1968 had changed their positions by 1972. All of this suggests that there are social forces at work that are altering women's basic perceptions of their work and family roles. That these attitude changes are reflected in actual behavior is evident from the analysis in several of the following chapters.

### Notes

1. The interviews with these young women have continued beyond the 1973 interview round. Relatively brief telephone interviews have been accomplished in 1975 and 1977, and a lengthy personal interview in early 1978. Additional interviews with this cohort will be carried out in 1980, 1982, and 1983. The National Longitudinal Surveys also include continuing interviews with three other cohorts: men forty-five to fifty-nine and fourteen to twenty-four years of age when first interviewed in 1966, and women aged thirty to forty-four years when first interviewed in 1967. See the Center for Human Resource Research, "The National Longitudinal Surveys Handbook" (mimeographed; Columbus: The Ohio State University, revised 1977) for a complete description of these surveys.

2. For a detailed description of the sampling, interviewing and estimating procedures, see the appendix. The overall sample also included 62 respondents of races other than white or black who are excluded in the analyses of this volume.

3. Because of the many social and economic differences between the black and white young women, virtually all of the discussion in this and subsequent chapters is based on separate racial analyses.

4. Two other factors normally considered to be associated with changes in labor force participation levels showed no significant association with changes in

work in overview tables and thus are not noted here. First, while substantial proportions of black and white women (24 and 33 percent, respectively) were living in a county in 1973 different than that in 1968, there were no differences in participation levels at this gross level of analysis. This issue is considered more carefully in chapter 6. Second, black and white women who evidenced a health condition in 1968 and 1973 had labor force rates not significantly different from women healthy at both points in time. For both races, the "ill-health" group is extremely small, representing only 2.7 percent of all white and 3.5 percent of all black women.

5. These are the only two years in which this series of work attitude items was asked. The question read as follows: "Now I'd like for you to think about a family where there is a mother, a father who works full time, and several children under school age. A trusted relative who can care for the children lives nearby. In this family situation, how do you feel about the mother taking a full time job outside the home? (a) If it is absolutely necessary to make ends meet, (b) If she prefers to work and her husband agrees, (c) If she prefers to work, but her husband does not particularly like it."

# 2 Young Women's Decisions to Attend College: Desires, Expectations, and Realizations

*Steven H. Sandell*

The extent of women's postsecondary schooling is an important aspect of their struggle for equality in the United States. Clearly, past educational achievements limit the accomplishments of adult women. Insofar as higher educational attainment implies greater labor force participation, lower unemployment, and higher earnings, the educational investment of young women foreshadows the probability of realizing these economic goals. Thus an examination of the education-related decisions of today's young women provides one basis for predicting their future position in American society.

The National Longitudinal Surveys show that while 78 percent of white and 76 percent of black young women in high school in 1968 expressed a desire to receive some higher education, only 52 percent of the white and 34 percent of the black young women actually entered college the year after their senior year in high school. Evaluating socioeconomic background and ability as determinants of college attendance is obviously crucial in establishing educational policy. For example, low entrance rates for persons from low-income families may suggest policies that would ease the financial burden of college attendance for these prospective students. Furthermore, examining the likelihood of college attendance for young women from various racial and ability groups is a necessary first step in evaluating the use of society's higher educational resources.

In this chapter we examine the college attendance decision of young women. More specifically, we analyze the effects of race, mental ability, parental education, and family income on the desired, expected, and actual college attendance of young women who were enrolled in high school in 1968, 1969, or 1970.

Economic theory prescribes a model for the individual's demand for college attendance. The developed framework demonstrates that if a woman chooses the quantity of her education to maximize the present value of her future earnings stream, the education decision will depend on her mental ability, on the educational attainment of her parents, and on her family's financial resources. For example, if women of higher ability can make better use of education, they are more likely to attend college. In addition, college admission standards limit the access of low-ability students to postsecondary institutions. Parental education is postively associated with young women's taste for education and

With the assistance of Rex C. Johnson and Julie Zavakos.

17

consequently with the probability of college attendance. Finally, if capital market imperfections make financing more expensive for women from low-income families, these individuals are less likely, on average, to attend college.

This chapter is organized in the following manner. The first section elaborates the economic model. In the following section, regression analysis is used to examine the young women's demands for postsecondary education. This section is followed by one advancing some conclusions.

### An Economic Model of Higher Education Enrollment

*The Decision to Attend College*

From an economic perspective, an individual will invest in a college education if the anticipated rate of return is higher than the costs of funds used in the investment.[1] In this framework, we can examine the effects of ability, differences in family financial circumstances and parental education, and tuition subsidies on the demand for places in college.

Number of years of schooling and ability are, according to Hause, complementary in affecting labor market earnings.[2] If women with greater ability can more easily convert an educational input into increased labor market productivity (hence, higher earnings), then the higher the person's native intelligence, the greater the rate of return to an incremental unit of education. Also, if scholarships are awarded on the basis of ability, persons with higher ability can reap a higher rate of return by obtaining the same education at a lower (private) direct cost.

Ability is occasionally a crucial aspect of a young woman's potential for entering specific institutions. Some colleges apparently deny admissions to some women who would be eager to attend. In economic terms, these colleges have excess demand for places in their freshman classes. Often the college rations the available places according to admissions requirements by selecting students on the basis of their ability or past achievements. Thus the ability of young women must be above a designated level before they are eligible to attend some institutions.

Imperfections in the financial capital market arise in part because human capital cannot serve as collateral and because considerable uncertainty exists about the future earnings of any given individual. If a person can finance her education from her own or her family's savings, exercising this option will reduce the cost of education, since the interest foregone for an incremental unit of funds is lower than the price she would have to pay for funds from commerical sources. Hence, the probability of college attendance should be positively correlated with parental family income and negatively correlated with family size.[3]

We anticipate a positive association between parental educational attainment and a young woman's acquisition of postsecondary education. First, it may reflect the parental influence on a young woman's acquired taste for higher education. Yet, more important with respect to financial considerations, parental education may affect the amount of subsidy the daughter will receive from any given family income. Thus, higher levels of parental education should enhance the probability of college attendance.

Since for any given level of postcollege earnings the rate of return for the investment in education is inversely related to the direct cost of college, tuition subsidies from state or private sources that lower the direct cost of a college education will have a positive effect on enrollment. In addition, such subsidies should have a greater positive inducement on the enrollment behavior of young women from poor families, since they are otherwise likely to finance their educations by borrowing.

**Empirical Analysis**

The empirical analysis involves estimating demand functions for college attendance. First, the determinants of desired and expected college attendance are examined for the young women who were high school students at the time of the initial survey in 1968. The factors influencing the fulfillment of these desires and expectations are then investigated using data on actual college attendance from the later surveys (1969-1971).

*The Demand for Higher Education*

The basic regression model for the decision to enroll in college is:

$$\text{College}_i = A + b\text{IQ}_i + c\text{Education}_i + d\text{Income}_i + f\text{Siblings}_i + u_i$$

where

| | |
|---|---|
| College$_i$ | is a dummy variable with the value of one if the respondent actually attends (or desires or expects to attend) college, and zero otherwise |
| $A$ | is a constant |
| IQ$_i$ | is a measure of the respondent's mental ability during high school |
| Education$_i$ | is the number of years of education of the respondent's father or head of household |

$\text{Income}_i$          is the income of the respondent's parental family[4]

$\text{Siblings}_i$       is the number of siblings of the respondent

$u_i$              represents the unexplained residual in the regression equation

$b, c, d,$ and $f$    represent the least squares regressors associated with $\text{IQ}_i$, $\text{Education}_i$, $\text{Income}_i$ and $\text{Siblings}_i$, respectively.[5]

Regression results for the three dependent variables presented in table 2-1 are generally consistent with economic theory. Young women from families with greater financial resources are likely to receive larger parental subsidies toward their college educations and consequently face a lower effective rate of interest on their investment. Hence, we expect and usually observe a negative effect of number of siblings and a positive effect of average family income on the desired, expected, and actual college attendance of white young women. For our sample of blacks, however, we observe an unexpected sign on the regression coefficient of number of siblings.

For some women marriage is apparently an alternative to college attendance. Hence, marital status the year following high school graduation is an inappropriate variable in a model that intends to explain college attendance. Restricting our analysis to women who were single the year after high school graduation supports this proposition. For this sample of whites, 57 percent, as opposed to 52 percent of the sample not controlled for marital status (see table 2-2), enrolled in college the year after completing high school. The corresponding proportions for blacks are 38 and 34 percent. Clearly, these are alternative sample specifications for the analysis. Since the decision to embark upon marriage is a young woman's choice, the remainder of our discussion refers to analyses of samples unrestricted by marital status.

As expected, for both racial groups we observe a significant positive effect of our measure of the respondent's mental ability. We interpret the positive coefficient for the mother's and father's educational attainment as representing the transmittal of a positive taste for education from parents to children.

To examine the effect of the mother's and father's educational attainment on the college attendance of their daughters, we entered these measures separately and jointly in the demand-for-college regressions. When we introduce mother's education into demand equations that include the father's education and family income as explanatory variables, the regression coefficients of these variables are reduced for whites. In contrast, the inclusion of the additional explanatory variable for blacks reduces the coefficient of the father's education but does not alter the family income coefficient. The most appropriate model specification is ambiguous with respect to parental education. In the remainder of this paper, mother's education is used exclusively.

Table 2-3 displays probabilities of desiring, expecting, and actually attending college for white young women, as computed from the regression analysis reported in table 2-1. These probabilities simplify and illuminate the implications of the analysis. For example, among white women with (1) two siblings, (2) a mother who has completed twelve years of schooling, and (3) a parental family income of $9,000, those with low ability (IQ = 90) are, on the average, about half as likely to attend college (36 versus 73 percent) as those with high ability (IQ = 130). Similarly, holding ability constant at IQ = 110 and examining the probability of attendance at various levels of average family income, we find that increasing income from $9,000 to $17,000 yields a modest increase of 8 percentage points in the probability of actually attending college.

Another interesting comparison is the difference in the behavior of the income variable in affecting the *desire* for college, the *expectation* of attending, and *actual attendance*. For a given IQ = 110, the difference between the probabilities of desiring and expecting college is .07 when family income is $9,000. However, this difference is only .03 for respondents whose average family income is $17,000. When we compare the difference in probability between expecting to attend college and actually attending, holding IQ constant at 110, this difference increases, on the average, as income increases. For the respondent coming from a $9,000 income family, the difference in probabilities is .18, whereas the difference is .20 for the respondent with an average family income of $17,000. While these differences are not large, they are systematic, suggesting a linkage between family income, attitude formation (the desire for college), and college attendance.

For a given ability, the differences in probabilities of desiring and actually attending college are highly stable as income varies. For a woman with an IQ of 90, the difference is about .28 regardless of the level of family income. For an IQ of 110, the difference is about .24 regardless of income. And, for an IQ of 130, this differential falls to about .20. Individuals from low-income families may simply be discouraged (perhaps erroneously) by the prospect of financing college attendance. This may also reflect fundamentally different attitudes concerning the value of education.

Table 2-3 also exhibits the corresponding mean probabilities for blacks. Assigning identical characteristics to both races enables us to compare racial differences in the effects of those characteristics on the dependent variables. These calculations indicate that black young women are more likely than their white counterparts to desire and expect college attendance for every income/ ability group. This observation also applies to all but one case in the probability of actually attending. Furthermore, the changes in probabilities due to change in income and ability differ in several respects from those observed for whites. For example, a 20 percentage point increment in IQ for blacks is associated with a 12 percentage point increase in the probability of desiring college, and a 15 percentage point increase in the probabilities of expecting and actually attending

**Table 2-1**
**Determinants of Desired, Expected, and Actual College Attendance for White and Black Young Women in High School in 1968: Regression Results[a]**
*(t Values in Parentheses)*

| Independent Variables | Dependent Variables | | | | | | | |
|---|---|---|---|---|---|---|---|---|
| | Desire College | Expect College | Actual College Attendance | Desire College | Expect College | Actual College Attendance | Actual College Attendance | Actual College Attendance |
| | Whites[b] | | | | | | | |
| Father's years of schooling completed | .033 (4.44)*** | | | .018 (3.11)*** | .026 (4.28)*** | .039 (5.84)*** | .028 (3.65)*** | |
| Mother's years of schooling completed | | .038 (4.77)*** | .049 (5.59)*** | | | | .032 (3.24)*** | .018 (5.30)*** |
| Average family income, 1967-70 (in 1967 dollars) | .007 (2.10)** | .012 (3.68)*** | .010 (2.63)*** | .007 (2.14)** | .011 (3.20)*** | .007 (1.77)** | .005 (1.20) | |
| Number of siblings in 1968 | -.012 (-1.44)* | -.014 (-1.66)** | -.010 (-1.05) | -.013 (-1.55)* | -.014 (-1.66)** | -.009 (-.96) | -.007 (-.76) | -.016 (-1.68)** |
| IQ x 0.01 | .719 (5.81)*** | .690 (5.25)*** | .942 (6.51)*** | .782 (6.34)*** | .743 (5.71)*** | .992 (6.96)*** | .914 (6.37)*** | 1.120 (7.74)*** |
| Constant | -.431 (-3.05) | -.570 (-3.80) | -1.154 (-6.99) | -.319 (-2.31) | -.472 (-3.24) | -1.056 (-6.62) | -1.194 (-7.29) | -.849 (-5.32) |
| $R^2$ (adjusted) | .15 | .17 | .20 | .13 | .17 | .20 | .21 | .16 |
| F ratio | 27.7*** | 33.3*** | 38.4*** | 24.8*** | 32.0*** | 39.3*** | 34.0*** | 38.8*** |

*Blacks*[b]

| | | | | | | | |
|---|---|---|---|---|---|---|---|
| Father's years of schooling completed | .019 (1.02) | .021 (1.06) | | .018 (1.43) | .030 (2.29)** | .044 (3.55)*** | .039 (2.87)*** | .039 (2.87)*** |
| Mother's years of schooling completed | | | .040 (2.15)** | | | | .015 (.75) | |
| Average family income, 1967-70 (in 1967 dollars) | .008 (.65) | 0.009 (.68) | .029 (2.37)*** | .003 (.24) | −.001 (−.04) | .017 (1.32)* | .017 (1.30)* | .035 (2.84)*** |
| Number of siblings in 1968 | .029 (2.00) | .021 (1.36) | .027 (1.85) | .027 (2.09) | .022 (1.65) | .025 (1.97) | .030 (2.10) | .011 (.86) |
| IQ x 0.01 | .599 (2.24)** | .742 (2.60)*** | .740 (2.72)*** | .694 (2.73)*** | .855 (3.19)*** | .946 (3.77)*** | .877 (3.27)*** | .916 (3.48)*** |
| Constant | −.157 (−.60) | −.334 (−1.21) | −1.032 (−3.91) | −.172 (−.70) | −.436 (−1.67) | −1.112 (−4.56) | −1.180 (−4.52) | −.754 (−3.23) |
| $R^2$ (adjusted) | .08 | .09 | .22 | .09 | .12 | .27 | .27 | .20 |
| F ratio | 3.55*** | 3.94*** | 9.37*** | 3.83*** | 5.10*** | 11.93*** | 9.62*** | 10.6*** |

aSummary statistics are reported in table 2-2.
bSample sizes for whites and blacks, respectively, are 612 and 118.

*Significant at the 10 percent level.
**Significant at the 5 percent level.
***Significant at the 1 percent level.

**Table 2-2**

**Means and Standard Deviations for Determinants of Desired, Expected, and Actual College Attendance**

*(Standard Deviations in Parentheses)*

| Variable Description | Whites in High School in 1968 | Blacks in HighSchool in 1968 |
|---|---|---|
| Desire college attendance (dummy coded 1 if the respondent desires education beyond high school) | .78 (.42) | .76 (.43) |
| Expect college attendance (dummy coded 1 if the respondent expects education beyond high school) | .72 (.45) | .69 (.46) |
| Actual college attendance (dummy coded 1 if the respondent attends college the year following grade 12) | .52 (.50) | .34 (.48) |
| Father's years of schooling completed | 11.68 (3.24) | 8.57 (3.62) |
| Mother's years of schooling completed | 11.76 (2.38) | 9.74 (2.71) |
| Average family income, 1967-1970 (in 1967 dollars) | 11,882.04 (5,568.28) | 6,449.30 (3,425.65) |
| IQ | 107.30 (13.22) | 89.02 (16.17) |
| Number of siblings in 1968 | 2.96 (1.97) | 5.11 (3.18) |
| Number of respondents | 612 | 118 |

college. For whites, the same improvement in ability is associated with 14, 13, and 18 percentage point increases in the probability of desiring, expecting, and actually attending college, respectively. For blacks, a $4,000 increase in family income, irrespective of the level of ability, increases the probability of attending college by 11 percentage points, whereas for whites, the increase is only 4 percentage points. On the other hand, a $4,000 increase in family income, regardless of the level of ability, increases the probability of desiring college by 3 percent for both racial groups.

Dividing the probability of actually attending college by the probability of desiring to attend college for each income/ability group yields statistics that illustrate the proportion of those persons desiring college who actually attend. Clearly, persons with higher family income and higher ability are more likely than other young women to realize their higher educational aspirations.

After conducting separate regression analyses of the determinants of actual college attendance for white young women who were high school seniors in 1968, 1969, and 1970, we observed different estimates of the demand-for-edu-

**Table 2-3**
**Probability of Desired, Expected, and Actual College Attendance for White and Black Young Women by Ability and Average Family Income[a]**

| IQ | Family Income = $9,000 | | | Family Income = $13,000 | | | Family Income = $17,000 | | |
|---|---|---|---|---|---|---|---|---|---|
| | Probability (Desire) | Probability (Expect) | Probability (Actual) | Probability (Desire) | Probability (Expect) | Probability (Actual) | Probability (Desire) | Probability (Expect) | Probability (Actual) |
| | | | | *Whites* | | | | | |
| IQ = 90 | .65 | .59 | .36 | .68 | .64 | .40 | .71 | .68 | .44 |
| IQ = 110 | .79 | .72 | .54 | .82 | .77 | .58 | .85 | .82 | .62 |
| IQ = 130 | .94 | .86 | .73 | .97 | .91 | .77 | .99 | .96 | .81 |
| | | | | *Blacks* | | | | | |
| IQ = 90 | .74 | .71 | .43 | .77 | .74 | .54 | .80 | .78 | .66 |
| IQ = 110 | .86 | .86 | .58 | .89 | .89 | .69 | .92 | .93 | .81 |
| IQ = 130 | .98 | 1.00 | .73 | 1.00 | 1.00 | .84 | 1.00 | 1.00 | .96 |

[a]Computations based on mother's education = twelve years, respondent's siblings = two years, and regression coefficients reported in table 2-1. Universe consists of women enrolled in high school in 1968. Calculated probabilities over 1.00 are reported as 1.00.

cation model for the three years, particularly between 1968 and 1969 on the one hand, and 1970 on the other.[6] Parental educational attainment (a taste factor) is apparently more important in 1968 than in 1970, while the variables representing the family's financial capacity (family income and number of siblings) are highly significant in 1970, although statistically indistinguishable from zero in 1968. Furthermore, the respondent's mental ability has a smaller effect on college attendance in 1970 than in the previous two years. We hypothesize that changing economic conditions over the period (higher inflation, unemployment, and interest rates) resulted in greater importance of family financial resources in college attendance decisions by 1970. To test this hypothesis, we produced a variant of the demand model that interacts a dummy variable indicating high-school senior status in 1970 with the variables for family income and number of siblings. We later included these interactions in a sample of all high-school students in 1968. Significance tests rejected the null hypothesis that the effects of the variables on 1970 seniors are indistinguishable from the effects on 1968 and 1969 seniors.[7] Thus we find support for the hypothesis that college attendance decisions are sensitive to short-run economic conditions.

Examining student expenditures with respect to (1) the respondent's ability, (2) her family's financial capacity, and (3) her mother's educational attainment enables us to make several meaningful observations. These observations relate to the amount that students from various income/ability levels pay for college education and how much the college is willing to subsidize them. For example, concentrating on net tuition, an additional $1,000 of family income is associated with $31 more in tuition expenditures by young women. A 10 percentage point increase in IQ is associated with an additional $62 in tuition expenses, while an additional year of mother's education produces a $47 increment in tuition paid by young women.

The difference between expenditure per student and tuition paid per student is the subsidy received by each student in attendance. This subsidy comes predominantly from tax revenue for public colleges, while a portion of the subsidy for private college students is obtained from private donations. This subsidy differs among students by sex, family income and ability. In 1967 dollars, the mean expenditure per student was $2,159 for men and $1,721 for women.[8] Since women paid an average net tuition of $653, compared to $694 for men, they received an average yearly subsidy of $1,068, compared to $1,465 for men. In addition, insofar as a greater subsidy corresponds with a greater financial capability for attending a higher quality (and generally more expensive) institution, these figures may further illuminate earnings differentials by sex. Since men, on average, attend higher quality colleges than women, controlling only for the number of years of education in earnings functions will tend to overstate the difference in male-female earnings. Furthermore, if our results apply to older cohorts of men and women, the finding that the return to education for married women is less than that for married men may be partially

attributed to differences in the quality of the education that women and
acquired.

## Conclusion

The decisions of young women to enter college are consistent with the economic
investment model. White women's desired, expected, and actual college attendance are positively related to their parents' educational attainment, family
income, and their own mental ability, and are negatively related to the number
of siblings. We obtained similar, but statistically weaker findings for black
women, with the exception of the effect of number of siblings. Furthermore, a
significant and positive relationship exists between young women's mental
ability, family income, and their expenditures on postsecondary education.

This study documents the importance of socioeconomic background as a
determinant of the education decisions of young women. Low family income is
associated with a lower probability of college attendance. Lower parental
earnings among blacks considerably explain the lower actual college attendance
for blacks than whites. Thus investment in college education by both white and
black women would apparently increase if financial constraints were lessened.

The data have supported the hypothesis that aggregate economic conditions
influence the demand for college attendance among young women. The amount
of family income available for financing education is significantly more important in the attendance decisions for high-school seniors in 1970 than in 1968 and
1969. We posit that this finding is the result of increasing uncertainty in family
finances over the period due to rising unemployment, inflation, and interest
rates.

Finally, the study documents the importance of parental educational
attainment as a factor affecting the desired, expected, and actual college
attendance of young women. If young women whose parents are not college
graduates do not receive the prerequisite encouragement and financial support
from their parental families to seek higher education, their teachers, their peers,
and perhaps the government have an important role to play.

## Notes

1. We assume that both the young woman and her parents make the college
investment decision. Of course, college attendance contains present and future
consumption benefits. We posit these benefits as independent of the investment
aspects and ignore them for the remainder of the present analysis.

2. See John C. Hause, "Earnings Profile: Ability and Schooling," *Journal of
Political Economy* 80 (May/June 1972, part 2): S108-138.

3. This is offset somewhat since scholarships and government-guaranteed low-interest loans are often awarded on the basis of need.

4. Since permanent income is a more appropriate measure of parental financial capacity than current income, our measure is the average reported family income in 1967 dollars for the available survey years.

5. We implicitly assume that the supply of places in college is infinitely elastic—that is, persons who are willing to make the requisite expenditure will be admitted to college. If the assumption is not valid, the interpretation of the regression coefficient for our measure of ability would be altered slightly, reflecting an admissions constraint. Other factors have been included in previous studies of educational aspirations and attainment. These include: high school curriculum, encouragement by parents and teachers, reading material in the home, high-school quality, etc. Since many of these variables introduce behavioral aspects (that is, students with greater ability receive more encouragement), they have been excluded from the simple economic model.

6. Too few sample cases preclude separate year analyses for black women.

7. The test for the difference in regression coefficients in the same estimating equation is:

$$t = \frac{C_A - C_B}{\sqrt{\mathrm{Var}_{C_A} + \mathrm{Var}_{C_B} - 2\,(\mathrm{Cov}_{C_A, C_B})}}$$

where

| | |
|---|---|
| $C_A$ and $C_B$ | are the two coefficients |
| $\mathrm{Var}_{C_A}$ and $\mathrm{Var}_{C_B}$ | are the variances of the respective coefficients |
| $\mathrm{Cov}_{C_A, C_B}$ | is the covariance between the two coefficients |

The source for this test is Henri Theil, *Principles of Econometrics* (New York: John Wiley and Sons, Inc., 1971), p. 138. Applying the test to the difference in the effect of family income on actual college attendance for 1970 seniors and 1968/1969 seniors yields a $t$ statistic of 2.136, which is significant at the 5 percent level (two-tail test). The same test for the difference in the effect of number of siblings yields a $t$ value of $-2.42$, significant at the 5 percent level.

8. For a more complete analysis of the acquisition of college quality see Steven H. Sandell, "The Demand for College Quality," mimeographed. Columbus: Center for Human Resource Research, The Ohio State University, 1977.

# 3

## Pregnancy, Motherhood, and Work Activity

*Frank L. Mott* and
*David Shapiro*

One major manifestation of the changing position of women in American society has been the increasing propensity of women at all ages to participate actively in the labor force. Indeed, the overall labor force participation rate for women has increased from 37.8 percent to 46.4 percent during the fifteen-year period between 1960 and 1975.[1]

Traditionally, women tended to work primarily in the years immediately after leaving school. They then withdrew from the labor force either when they married or as they approached the birth of their first child. Some women would subsequently return to the work force when their last child reached school age; others would remain out of the labor force. In recent years, this traditional pattern has been changing. Higher proportions of women are returning to the labor force and increasing proportions of young women, in connection with the birth of their children, are remaining out of the labor force for only short periods of time. As a result, between 1960 and 1975, the labor force participation rate for women with children under the age of three more than doubled from 15.3 to 34.4 percent.[2]

While female labor force participation levels at all life-cycle points are higher than they have been in past decades, the birth of the first child still remains a major transition point for many women. Reflecting the birth event and the subsequent presence of an infant, substantial numbers of young women withdraw from the labor force. However, as our data demonstrate, this phenomenon is apparently of a more temporary nature than has been true in the past. The average woman now stays in the labor force until three or four months before the birth and, in many instances, returns soon after the birth (figure 3-1).

This chapter has several objectives, all of which are related to the overriding objective of clarifying, both descriptively and analytically, the patterns of labor force withdrawal and reentry associated with the first birth. First, patterns of labor force activity surrounding this birth are described in greater detail than has hitherto been possible. Then, since a young woman's ideas about childbearing may represent a somewhat longer time perspective, the patterns of her current labor force activity are examined within the context of her fertility ideals and expectations. That is, if there is a consistency between current work patterns and prospective fertility behavior, it is not unreasonable to hypothesize a certain

The authors wish to thank Jean Haurin for her outstanding research assistance on this chapter.

29

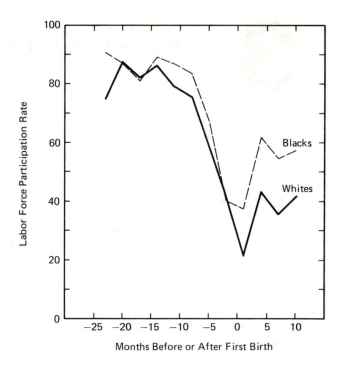

Note: Limited to respondents not enrolled in school at relevant life-cycle points.

**Figure 3-1**. Labor Force Participation Rates Before and After First Birth by Race

common causality. Thus, if women with lower fertility expectations are also more likely to be working in the months immediately following their first birth, this evidenced consistency is suggestive of higher probabilities of working for these young women in the years ahead.

The concluding sections focus on interpreting young women's labor force activity, both cross sectionally and longitudinally, from a more straightforward economic perspective. The discussion will focus on suggesting ways in which varying disciplinary perspectives from both economics and sociology may be useful for interpreting divergent patterns of work activity between whites and blacks and between women from different socioeconomic origins.

**The Data Set**

Constraints imposed by the available data necessitate using different subsets of women for the two distinctly different analyses within this chapter. The section of the analysis focusing on labor force and fertility interaction uses responses to questions from the 1971 survey concerning the number of children that the women expect to have as well as the number of children that they consider ideal. Thus the reference point for that part of the analysis is the 1971 interview date. Also, since analogies are drawn between that research and the research described in the remaining sections of the chapter that focus on women before and after the first birth, the analysis of fertility ideals and expectations is limited to women with exactly one child.

In both the descriptive overview section and the section that provides the analysis of the labor force activity of these young women, virtually all the analyses focus on the 1,405 women in the sample who had their first birth at some point between the 1968 and 1973 interviews.[3] The data set for these analyses was constructed by using a pooled cross-section technique. On any given interview date, a woman's status in relationship to her first birth can be determined by matching the interview date with the date of birth of her first child. For example, if she was interviewed on March 1, 1969, and her first birth was on April 1, 1970, she was thirteen months (−13 months) before her first birth at her 1969 interview. Similarly, her status in relationship to her first birth can be measured as of every interview date between 1968 and 1973. The particular woman in the preceding example might have been twenty-five months before her first birth at the 1968 interview, thirteen months before the birth in 1969, one month before in 1970, eleven months after the first birth in 1971, and so forth.[4] On every one of the interview dates, we not only are aware of the woman's precise fertility status but, in addition, we also have a considerable amount of information about her work status. From this example, it should be apparent that many of the women in the sample could provide detailed labor force status information for several interview dates before and after the first birth. Thus, the 1,405 women who had a first birth between 1968 and 1973 were able to provide an effective sample that included many more than 1,405 points in time. Because of this, it was possible to develop a large and highly detailed work pattern for women, not only at all stages of pregnancy, but also for every month immediately following the birth of a first child.[5]

Finally, one brief section of this chapter uses the panel dimensions of the data set and compares young women's wages on their first job after their first birth with their last job before the birth. Here, job characteristics for the same women before and after the birth are matched. Thus, whereas the pooled data used for most of the research of this chapter compare *different* women at various points before and after the first birth, the comparison of wage focuses on identical individuals at two points in time.

## Labor Force Behavior Surrounding the First Birth:
## A Descriptive Overview

The months surrounding the first birth represent the life-cycle point when female labor force participation rates are at a minimum. As may be noted in figure 3-1, labor force participation levels for black and white women begin a decline during the early months of pregnancy. From rates approaching 80 percent at the beginning of pregnancy, they drop to 50 percent about three to four months before the birth, and plummet to 20 percent for whites and 40 percent for blacks near the birth event.[6] Note that, while the rates do indeed decline sharply in the months preceding the birth, nonetheless at virtually all points there are substantial numbers of women who choose to remain in the labor force.

This fact should be mediated by the knowledge that, in the months immediately surrounding the birth event, actual work activity is significantly below labor force participation levels. As may be noted in figure 3-2 for black and white women, the actual proportion of women at work in the month following the birth is below 10 percent, even though the percentage employed (with a job and either at work or not at work) is around 20 percent. The labor force participation rates at that point are even higher—close to 40 percent for black women and a little over 20 percent for white women.

Following the birth event, black and white labor force participation rates begin to rise. White labor force participation rates rise to approximately the 40 percent level, whereas black rates increase to between 50 and 60 percent. However, as is shown in figure 3-3, a not inconsequential part of the difference between the black and white rates reflects higher levels of black unemployment. Before as well as after the birth, many more black women are seeking, but are unable to find work.

In addition to the fact that the average black woman is more likely to be working or looking for work, there are major racial differences in the extent of postbirth labor force attachment. As is noted in figure 3-4, although there are no significant differences in average hours worked between employed (and at-work) black and white women before the birth, the average employed black woman is much more likely to be working full time (thirty-five hours or more) after the birth. Whereas the percentage of white women working full time after the birth is between 50 and 55, nearly 70 percent of employed black women are working full time immediately after the birth, and the rate rises to about 80 percent within a year after the birth.

The overall racial contrast in figure 3-1 disguises some major variations by educational levels. In figure 3-5, there are distinct differences in participation levels between the different race-education groups in the prebirth interval, as labor force rates are lowest for the black and white respondents with less than twelve years of school. After the birth, black women with twelve or more years of school return to the labor force in substantially greater proportions than do any of the other groups. At six months after the birth, over 60 percent of black women with at least a high-school diploma are in the labor force, compared with about 50 percent for black dropouts and about 40 percent for the two white education categories. The average black woman with twelve or more years of

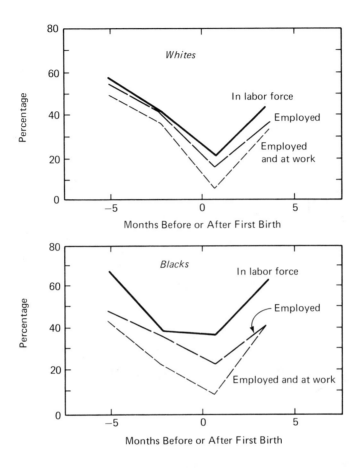

Note: Limited to respondents not enrolled in school at relevant life-cycle point.

**Figure 3-2** Percentage in Labor Force, Percentage Employed, and Percentage Employed and at Work Before and After First Birth by Race

school spends about eight months without a job due to the birth, compared with between thirteen and eighteen months for the other race-education groups.

It is also of some interest to note (figure 3-5) that the group with the second highest postbirth participation levels and propensity to return rapidly are the blacks with less than twelve years of school, suggesting generally higher levels of black labor force participation following the first birth. All of the preceding data suggest that there are distinct variations by race in labor force behavior following the first birth.

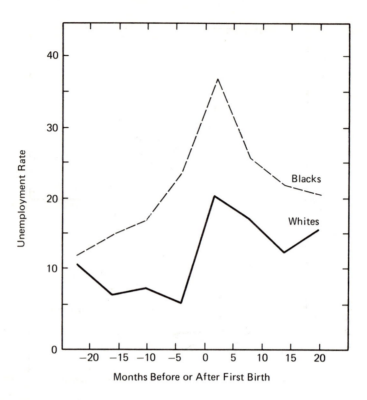

Note: Limited to respondents not enrolled in school at relevant life-cycle point.

**Figure 3-3.** Unemployment Rates Before and After First Birth by Race

### Some Perspectives on Labor Force and
### Fertility Interaction

Without belaboring the question of the direction of causality between fertility and labor force behavior, it seems reasonable to suggest that a young woman's decisions concerning fertility and work will be made within a common framework—that is, a woman may be expected to make decisions concerning her future fertility behavior that are consistent with her prospective and current labor force behavior as well as with her other economic circumstances.[7] Thus one can hypothesize that, everything else being equal, greater fertility expectations will be associated with a lesser propensity to work.

The preceding section showed higher levels of labor force participation for blacks as compared with whites. Fertility expectation data are generally consistent with the labor force data, as young one-parity black women have

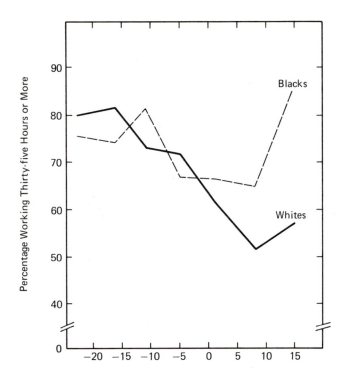

Note: Limited to respondents not enrolled in school at relevant life-cycle point. Also, the denominator references the actual hours worked in the relevant survey week.

**Figure 3-4.** Percentage Working Thirty-five Hours or More per Week of Respondents Employed and at Work Before and After First Birth by Race

distinctly lower fertility expectations than their white counterparts.[8] Whereas about one out of eight white women with one child do not expect additional children, the comparable statistic for black women is one out of three.

Some of the factors that differentially affect female black and white labor force participation (and, presumably, fertility behavior) are found within a standard economic labor-supply framework in the following section. However, there are certain aspects of the racial differential that may be interpreted more readily by incorporating several temporal dimensions. First, at all education levels, black young women come from poorer backgrounds than white young women. Thus to the extent that newly formed young families are able to gain an economic foothold through intergenerational transfer payments, young white families would probably, on the average, be more favorably endowed.

Also, the largest intergenerational disparities are for young black women

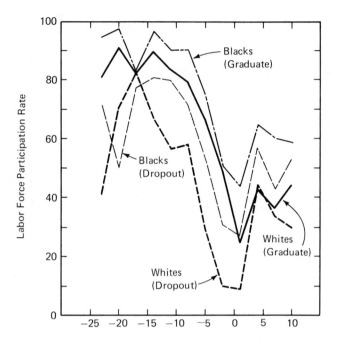

Note: Limited to respondents not enrolled in school at relevant life cycle point.

**Figure 3-5.** Labor Force Participation Rates Before and After First Birth by Educational Attainment and Race

with the highest education; less than 30 percent of white young women with some college have fathers with less than a high school degree, compared with almost two-thirds for young black women. Thus, to the extent that young women obtain financial assistance from their parents' generation, we expect the greatest *relative* handicap to exist among the better educated black women.

In addition to this intergenerational dimension, the average young black married woman at any educational level is likely to have a husband who has less education than the husband of her white counterpart. As with the intergenerational pattern, the largest educational discrepancy in this regard was for those women who had attended college. Among black college educated women, 63 percent were married to men with less than a high school diploma, compared with 28 percent for their white counterparts. Since a husband's education is directly associated with his current and prospective earnings, the average young black woman would have a greater need to work (and concomitantly, reduce fertility behavior) to attain a given family income level. Also, to the extent that black young mothers are more likely to be either separated, divorced, or never married, there is a greater incentive for the black woman to work. Indeed, as of the time of the first birth, 46 percent of the black women fell in the "no husband present" category, compared with only 10 percent of the white women.

Further, black husbands within a given educational category earned less than their white counterparts. All of these factors are consistent with the higher working propensities and lower fertility expectations of young black mothers compared with young white mothers. As a result of the same factors, black families at all educational levels are less likely to have money in savings accounts than their white counterparts. At the higher educational levels, black families are more likely than white families to have accumulated debts, reflecting in part the possibility of a greater relative gap in intergenerational mobility for black daughters compared with white daughters. That is, the higher debt level among the better educated blacks may be one manifestation of an upward mobility syndrome whereby they are striving, in spite of a less advantaged background, to reach the level of well-being of their better educated white counterparts.[9]

Table 3-1 shows that, even though the average black woman expects fewer children, she has higher fertility ideals than her white counterpart. To the extent that fertility ideals come closer to representing what a woman (and her husband) would *like* to do, racial differences between expectations and ideals may represent the relatively greater constraining effect of lower current and anticipated income levels on expected fertility for blacks than for whites.

The preceding discussion has focused on interrelationships between fertility expectations and labor force attachment, with considerable emphasis on black/white differences. Much of the remaining analysis in this chapter focuses on

**Table 3-1**
**Relationship Between Fertility Expectations and Fertility Ideals in 1971 by Race[a]**

*(Percentage Distributions)*

| Relationship Between Expectations and Ideals | Number of Respondents | Total Percent | One Child | Two Children | Three or More Children |
|---|---|---|---|---|---|
| | | *Whites* | | | |
| Expectations | 556 | 100.0 | 12.0 | 48.8 | 39.2 |
| Ideals | 556 | 100.0 | 3.4 | 59.9 | 36.7 |
| Difference | | | +8.6 | −11.1 | +2.5 |
| | | *Blacks* | | | |
| Expectations | 241 | 100.0 | 28.8 | 40.6 | 30.9 |
| Ideals | 241 | 100.0 | 6.9 | 47.5 | 45.6 |
| Difference | | | +21.9 | −6.9 | −14.7 |

[a]The universe is restricted to one-parity respondents who were not enrolled in school in 1971.

explaining the levels of and variations in female labor supply in the periods immediately preceding and following the birth of the first child.

## Work and Motherhood: An Economic Framework

Factors affecting the labor force participation of women have been subjected to considerable analysis by economists and sociologists. Here we use the labor supply framework of economics in an effort to determine if those factors generally found to be important determinants of female labor force participation are also relevant to participation decisions for the periods just before and after the first birth.

The labor supply framework of economics begins by positing that households will attempt to maximize utility. In the most simple formulation, a household will seek to maximize the utility derived from its (joint) consumption of income and leisure. The household must give up leisure time to earn income in the labor market.

In addition to leisure, however, there are obviously other important alternative uses of an individual's time (besides work in the labor market), such as work in the home and schooling.[10] To earn income in the market the household must give up time that would otherwise be spent in leisure and/or work in the home. Conversely, if one member of the household works and earns a relatively high income in the market, that income may be used (in part) to "purchase" more time for nonmarket uses for other household members.

In examining factors affecting a young woman's decision concerning labor force participation, the preceding discussion suggests that other household income (more precisely, family income less respondent's earnings) will be an important consideration—that is, in households where other family income is relatively high, we expect a greater likelihood that the respondent will not be in the labor force, everything else being equal. In effect, such households will be able to "buy" more time for leisure and/or work in the home than less affluent households.[11]

If a woman chooses not to work in the labor market, she bears an opportunity cost—that is, time spent out of the labor market represents foregone earnings. The greater a young woman's earning power (potential wage rate) in the labor market, the greater will be the opportunity cost of nonparticipation. Thus, we hypothesize that, other things being equal, a young woman's potential wage rate will be related positively to the likelihood that she is in the labor force at any point, since greater earning power implies that nonparticipation in the labor force is more costly.[12]

Apart from differences in other family income and (own) potential earning power, young women also may have differing tastes—different preferences among income, leisure, work in the home, and work in the market. While we cannot measure these tastes directly, we do make use of information from the National Longitudinal Surveys (NLS) concerning the respondent's educational attainment and expectations of future labor force attachment. These variables should serve as proxy measures for tastes. Educational attainment is correlated with the respondent's potential wage rate, and probably with other family income. However, since these variables are already controlled for in our model, we view the independent effect of educational attainment on labor force participation as reflecting a taste effect. Previous empirical work has suggested that greater educational attainment is positively related to tastes for market work, everything else being equal, since educational attainment is positively related to labor force participation.[13] At the same time, some recent evidence has been presented in the literature suggesting that better educated mothers tend to spend more time at home caring for young children.[14] Thus we hypothesize that prior to the first birth educational attainment will be positively related to labor force participation. After the birth, we have no strong hypothesis concerning the independent effects of education on participation.

The NLS data provide responses to questions concerning what respondents would like to be doing when they reach age thirty-five. We make use of these responses as an additional taste factor—that is, those young women who indicated that they would like to be working in the labor market at thirty-five are expected to have greater labor force participation rates.[15]

The labor supply framework of economics leads us to focus on the effects of other family income, respondent's earning power in the labor market, and tastes as determinants of labor force participation. Race per se does not explicitly enter into this framework. As noted previously, however, there are distinct racial differences in fertility expectations that are consistent with higher labor force attachment among blacks. It was suggested that these differences might be due in part to lower current and anticipated income levels for blacks.[16]

As noted earlier, young black women generally come from lower income backgrounds than their white counterparts. To the extent that this difference in family backgrounds is reflected in smaller intergenerational wealth transfers among blacks, one should observe higher labor force participation rates, other things being equal. Similarly, the fact that black one-parity women are less likely to be married with spouse present than their white counterparts also suggests that the black women will have higher participation rates. Overall, we believe that differences by race in terms of the factors just mentioned, when coupled with differences in the values of the other variables that are explicitly included in the analysis, result in labor force participation rates that are higher for blacks than for whites.

Further, it was noted that the black-white differences in upward mobility and debt tend to be greatest among those at the highest education level. Thus while upward mobility is generally greater for blacks than for whites, the interracial difference in mobility is greatest among the most highly educated. We hypothesize, therefore, that blacks who are relatively well off (college educated, relatively high income level) are most likely to be striving to move up the socioeconomic ladder. In such a situation fertility limitation would be a plausible means of raising the household's level of material well-being, and female labor force participation in affected households should be high. Empirically, this mobility hypothesis translates into expectations of high levels of female labor force participation among blacks with more education and with relatively high "other" family income, everything else being equal.

These hypotheses will be tested by means of multiple classification analysis (MCA), a version of multiple regression analysis with the explanatory variables expressed in categorical form. The MCA technique permits one to calculate the mean value of the dependent variable for each category of a particular explanatory variable "adjusted" for the effects of all other variables in the model. Differences in these adjusted values among the several categories of a given variable may be interpreted as indicating the "pure" effect of that variable on the dependent measure. To provide a specific example, the MCA technique calculates for each educational category of women that proportion of the category which would be in the labor force if those women were "average" in terms of all the other variables entering into the analysis. In the analysis that follows, we examine our hypotheses by focusing on these "adjusted" proportions.

*Some Multivariate Results*

We focus here on the major hypotheses set forth in the preceding section. The key variables are other family income, respondent's potential wage rate, and the principle proxy measure for taste—educational attainment. Figures 3-6 through 3-8 highlight the results for these key variables. (The interested reader who wishes to examine the total model can receive the overall results from the authors.)

The dependent variable in these estimates is labor force participation in the following periods before and after the first birth:

1. Labor force participation thirteen to eighteen months before the birth (1 = in labor force, 0= not in labor force)
2. Labor force participation six to twelve months before the birth
3. Labor force participation zero to five months before the birth
4. Labor force participation one to five months after the birth
5. Labor force participation six to twelve months after the birth

Other family income was hypothesized earlier to be inversely related to the likelihood that a young white woman would be in the labor force at any point in

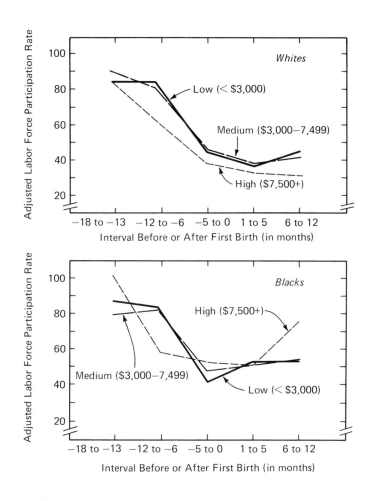

**Figure 3-6.** Adjusted Labor Force Participation Rates by Income Less Respondent's Earnings (Adjusted to 1967 Dollars) and Race

time. It is apparent from figure 3-6 that the data do provide some support for this hypothesis. More precisely, while there are no consistent differences in participation levels between the low- and middle-income groups, the high-income group does have consistently lower participation, other things being equal. The difference in (adjusted) participation levels narrows as the birth is approached, and then widens following the birth, since participation among low- and middle-income families begins to increase while participation in high-income households remains quite low. Thus it appears that among whites, high-income households "buy" more time for work in the home than less affluent house-

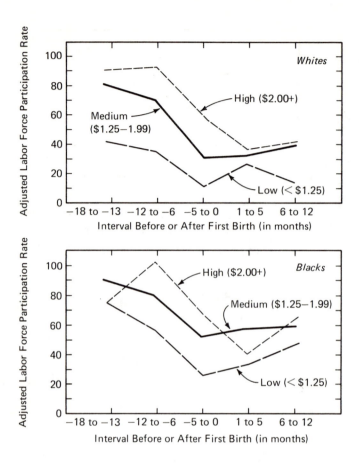

**Figure 3-7.** Adjusted Labor Force Participation Rates by Potential Hourly Wage (Adjusted to 1967 Dollars) and Race

holds, particularly in the early stages of pregnancy and after the birth. Among blacks, there is no evidence of an inverse relationship between participation and other family income. In fact, more than five months after the birth the highest (adjusted) labor force rates for blacks are those of the high-income group (figure 3-6). In comparing white and black rates by income group, it is apparent that after the birth blacks have generally higher participation rates. The differential by race is widest among the high-income group. These results are consistent with the mobility hypothesis proposed here.

The respondent's potential wage rate was hypothesized to be positively related to her labor force participation. The data provide considerable support

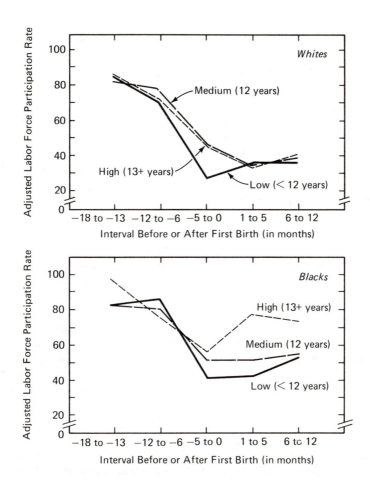

**Figure 3-8.** Adjusted Labor Force Participation Rates by Educational Attainment and Race

for this hypothesis. The potential wage rate is highly significant in almost all the intervals for whites and the pattern is generally in the expected direction for blacks, although the variable is not as highly significant as for whites. Figure 3-7 shows the adjusted labor force rates by potential wage rate. Among whites, moving from the low-wage to the high-wage group is associated with increased labor force participation in each of the five intervals. It appears that the high-wage group is much more likely to remain in the labor force until just before the birth, and this group is also more likely to return to the labor force after the birth.[17] Among blacks, the pattern of higher participation associated with a higher potential wage is generally present. Thus even though we are considering an important transitional period in the lives of these young women, it appears that their labor force behavior before and after the first birth is quite responsive to variations in the opportunity cost of nonmarket time.

Educational attainment was hypothesized to be positively related to labor force participation prior to the birth as a reflection of stronger tastes for market work. We had no strong hypothesis concerning the independent effect of education on participation following the birth. The mobility hypothesis suggests a stronger positive relationship among blacks. The *unadjusted* relationship between education and participation is quite strong. In every interval, for both whites and blacks, greater education is associated with higher participation. As suggested earlier, however, much of this association may reflect the positive correlation between education and the potential wage. Indeed, after controlling for the effects of the potential wage and other factors in the model, the overwhelmingly positive relationship between educational attainment and labor force participation is no longer present. For whites and blacks, the adjusted labor force rates by educational attainment are shown in figure 3.8.

Among whites, there is some support for the hypothesis that education and participation will be positively related prior to the birth. The low-education group has distinctly lower (adjusted) participation during pregnancy—particularly so in the interval immediately preceding the birth. In the interval immediately following the birth, participation rates (both adjusted and unadjusted) are nearly identical for all three educational attainment groups. Thus, comparison of these two intervals indicates that, other things being equal, the presence of an infant has a greater depressing effect on the labor force participation of the better educated young white mothers.

Contrary to the pattern among whites, schooling is not consistently related to participation of blacks prior to the birth, but there is a generally positive relationship between schooling and (adjusted) participation after the birth. In comparing whites and blacks at comparable schooling levels, it is apparent that blacks have higher labor force rates. In addition, the racial difference is widest among the college educated. This result is quite consistent with our earlier discussion focusing on the high upward mobility and debt accumulation among blacks with college education.

To summarize, we began this section by drawing on the analytical framework of economics and hypothesizing that, other things being equal, labor force participation would be inversely related to other family income and positively related to the respondent's earning power in the labor market as well as (to some extent) to her educational attainment. We also focused on racial differences in family background and in some of the variables included directly in the analysis. This framework helps explain why blacks have generally higher participation rates than whites. It also led us to hypothesize that the relatively greater upward mobility of well-educated, higher-income blacks would strengthen the expectation of a positive relationship between education and participation and weaken the expected inverse relationship between other family income and participation.

In general, the data provide support for most of these hypotheses. More precisely, black participation rates are generally greater than those of whites, with the greatest differences following the birth of the first child. For both blacks and whites, the single most powerful variable influencing labor force participation before and after the birth is the potential wage rate. Other family income is somewhat inversely related to participation among whites, during pregnancy and after the birth. Among blacks there is no clear relationship prior to the birth and more than five months after the birth the highest (adjusted) participation is by the high-income group. For whites, but not for blacks, there is some evidence of a positive relationship between educational attainment and prebirth participation, other things being equal. However, after the birth there is a strong positive relationship among blacks, but no pronounced pattern for whites. Thus, while the data do provide support for the implications of conventional labor supply analysis, we also note the presence of interracial differences in the effects of schooling and other family income (particularly after the birth) that are quite consistent with our discussion of mobility effects.

### The Effect of Employment Discontinuity on Wages

The discussion in this chapter has focused primarily on the differential propensities of women to maintain an attachment to the labor force in the periods before and after the birth of their first child. We have found distinct differences in participation levels by race, by earning power in the labor market, and, to a lesser degree, by educational attainment and household income level. At least in part, we have interpreted the racial differentials as being due to differences in levels of other family income, marital status, and savings and debt accumulation that partially reflect racial differentials in intergenerational mobility patterns.

Whereas the earlier sections contrast women who are in the labor force with those who are not, this analysis focuses only on women who return to the labor force after the birth. More specifically, some women are better able to regain or improve on the wage level of their prebirth job than others. Here we briefly examine the factors that appear to be related to changes in wages among these "early returnees."

Overall, black and white women who returned to the work force were surprisingly successful in recouping and improving on their prebirth wage. White women, on the average, attained an hourly wage on their first postbirth job 11 percent above that of their last prebirth job; black women did even better, averaging a 17 percent increase (all wages are adjusted to 1967 dollars). Part of these significant increases undoubtedly reflected the occurrence of a "selecting out" process, whereby those women who were able to find a job that provided an above-average wage were more likely to return to work.[18] The somewhat better ability of blacks to improve on their prebirth wage level should be tempered by the knowledge that their average prebirth wage was well below that of their white counterparts. Blacks earned, on the average, $1.34 an hour compared with $1.78 for white respondents.

To examine more carefully the variations among different subgroups in the ability to retain or improve on prebirth wages, multiple classification analyses regressing wage change on a number of personal and prebirth job-related characteristics were performed (table 3-2). After controlling for prebirth wage levels, it is evident that better educated women are best able to improve on their prebirth wages. Whereas black and white high-school dropouts, on the average, exactly attained their prebirth wage level, white women with at least a high-school diploma improved their wages by over 10 percent, and their black counterparts showed a 25 percent increase. The substantial improvement for better educated black women is consistent with our earlier discussions, which highlighted the fact that these women were more likely to return to the labor force than any other race-education group. The more successful that women in a particular group expect to be in their labor market search in terms of maintaining or improving on an earlier job position, the more likely they will be to seek employment.

In addition, women whose absence from employment (associated with childbearing) was relatively brief tended to be more successful at improving on earlier wage levels, as shown by the fact that fewer months between "last" and "first" jobs is generally associated with better wage retention. This is consistent with the notion that a shorter period of absence not only is associated with a smaller depreciation of specific and general skills acquired on earlier jobs, but in addition, probably reflects closer continuing ties with the job market.[19] A woman who is absent from work for a relatively brief time probably, on the average, still has better personal job contacts and a greater awareness of available employment opportunities.

Class of worker at last prebirth job was included in the analysis because we hypothesized that civil service provisions and (perhaps) more liberal maternity-leave policies in the public sector would result in government workers being better able to retain their prebirth wage levels. There is little evidence to support this hypothesis, however.

## Conclusion

The results of this chapter are suggestive of continuing dramatic increases in labor force participation levels at that life-cycle point where women, for the most part, have traditionally withdrawn from market work activities. Clearly,  young women now stay in the labor force until they are within a few months of the birth of their first child and frequently return to the labor force shortly after the birth. This is particularly true for black women.

Reflecting both a relatively short interval away from work as well as the likelihood that women with better job options appear to be the first ones to return, most of the women who do return within a brief time span are relatively successful in at least regaining their prebirth wages. In many instances they may return at wage levels substantially above those of their prebirth jobs.

From a policy perspective, all of the preceding analysis suggests that both in- and out-of-school guidance, training, and education should be aimed at assisting young women in planning for work careers that will probably be substantially continuous, rather than following the traditional modal pattern of postschool work, extensive interruption for childbearing and childrearing, and perhaps a return to work when the children reach school age. The average young woman in high school (or college) may not be cognizant of contemporary realities. Thus guidance programs should emphasize the likely short-term work interruption that young women now encounter, and education and training programs should be geared toward patterns of continuing, rather than widely intermittent, lifetime employment.

The results of this chapter present a mixed picture concerning the ability of women at this life-cycle stage to be successful in the labor market. We have demonstrated that the unemployment rate for white women reaches 20 percent, and for black women exceeds 30 percent in the months following the first birth, even though virtually all of these women have had recent labor market experience. On the other hand, we have also shown that those who do find jobs often are quite successful.

Generally speaking, the employment-related experiences of these women parallel the experiences of the adult population at large—that is, those with less education and skills have disproportionate difficulty finding employment and attaining satisfactory wages. The most satisfactory adjustments are made by those with the most education. This is particularly true for black women.

It appears that better institutional means are necessary for helping many of these young women—particularly those with less education and work-related skills—with their reentry problems, as well as ensuring maximum compliance with maternity-related employment provisions. Where these provisions are inadequate, perhaps stronger employment provisions are needed for ensuring more equitable wages, hours, and working conditions for this increasingly important segment of the American labor force.

From a research perspective, it is apparent that the lifetime work orientation of women is gradually approaching the more continuous pattern followed by men. As such, theoretical economic modeling of female labor force participation—both short and long term—may in the years ahead be more closely

**Table 3-2**
Unadjusted and Adjusted Ratios[a] of Hourly Rate of Pay at First Postbirth Job to Hourly Rate of Pay at Last Prebirth Job by Race: Multiple Classification Analysis[b]

| Characteristics | Whites | | | | Blacks | | | |
|---|---|---|---|---|---|---|---|---|
| | Number of Respondents | Unadjusted Ratio | Adjusted Ratio | F Ratio | Number of Respondents | Unadjusted Ratio | Adjusted Ratio | F Ratio |
| Same employer | | | | 2.29 | | | | .53 |
| Yes | 142 | 107 | 108 | | 64 | 104 | 122 | |
| No or not ascertainable | 221 | 114 | 114 | | 146 | 122 | 114 | |
| Hourly rate of pay at last prebirth job (adjusted to 1967 dollars) | | | | 27.95*** | | | | 9.28*** |
| $0-1.49 | 103 | 132 | 134 | | 117 | 134 | 135 | |
| $1.50-1.99 | 121 | 105 | 107 | | 50 | 102 | 102 | |
| $2.00 or more | 139 | 102 | 98 | | 43 | 88 | 85 | |
| Highest grade of schooling completed | | | | 3.30** | | | | 3.68** |
| 0-11 | 59 | 111 | 99 | | 77 | 116 | 101 | |
| 12 | 207 | 113 | 114 | | 105 | 119 | 128 | |
| 13-18 | 97 | 107 | 112 | | 28 | 110 | 123 | |
| Occupation on last prebirth job | | | | 2.71** | | | | .20 |
| Professional/managerial | 59 | 110 | 120 | | 13 | 93 | 115 | |
| Clerical/sales | 177 | 105 | 106 | | 80 | 116 | 122 | |
| Service | 66 | 125 | 117 | | 52 | 124 | 113 | |
| Other | 61 | 113 | 110 | | 65 | 117 | 115 | |
| Class of worker at last prebirth job | | | | .53 | | | | .79 |
| Private | 308 | 111 | 111 | | 160 | 119 | 119 | |
| Public | 55 | 111 | 115 | | 50 | 108 | 109 | |
| Enrollment status | | | | 3.45* | | | | 9.77*** |
| Enrolled | 49 | 126 | 120 | | 72 | 137 | 137 | |
| Not enrolled | 314 | 109 | 110 | | 138 | 106 | 106 | |

Number of months between prebirth and postbirth jobs

| | N | | | F | N | | | F |
|---|---|---|---|---|---|---|---|---|
| 0-6 | 184 | 111 | 118 | | 83 | 107 | 112 | |
| 7-12 | 64 | 115 | 110 | | 52 | 125 | 126 | |
| 13-24 | 74 | 109 | 102 | | 58 | 123 | 118 | |
| 25 or more | 41 | 111 | 100 | 4.21*** | 17 | 123 | 107 | .53 |
| Grand mean | 363 | 111 | 111 | 4.98*** | 210 | 117 | 117 | 2.21*** |
| $R^2$ (adjusted) | | | | .13 | | | | .07 |

[a]Ratios are multiplied by 100.

[b]Universe consists of women employed before and after the birth of their first child.

*Significant at the 10 percent level.

**Significant at the 5 percent level.

***Significant at the 1 percent level.

approximated by the standard theoretical perspectives previously appropriate only for diagnosing male work activity.


**Notes**

1. Howard Hayghe, "Marital and Family Characteristics of the Labor Force in March 1973," *Monthly Labor Review* 97 (April 1974):21-27; and "Marital and Family Characteristics of the Labor Force, March 1975," *Monthly Labor Review* 98 (November 1975):52-55.

2. Ibid.

3. By focusing on the one-parity group, we are relating information for a group of women who, for the most part, can be assumed to be fecund. Thus expectations for this specific group may be assumed to be maximally associated with prospective reality to the extent that expectations are indeed associated with subsequent fertility behavior.

4. From the perspective of the postfirst-birth analyses in this chapter, a woman is considered as having a postfirst-birth status only until she has her second birth. Thus, if on a given interview date a woman already has had her second birth, *that particular interview date* is no longer considered within scope for this particular analysis for that woman. Of course, if earlier interview dates preceded the second birth, those points in time were included in this analysis. Also, the analysis was limited to women who were not enrolled in school on the relevant interview dates. For more details, see appendix 3A.

5. A comparison of labor force participation curves for women having their first birth at different points during the five-year period indicates no apparent bias from using this technique.

6. The interested reader may note that labor force participation rates, employment rates, and unemployment rates cited in this chapter are systematically several points higher than estimates for comparable population groups in the decennial census. This is true for both black and white respondents. While exactly comparable population groups to those used in this chapter cannot be found in any census or Current Population Survey, crude comparisons can be made by comparing NLS and 1970 Census (U.S. Bureau of the Census, Census of Population: 1970, Final Report PC(2)-6A, *Employment Status and Work Experience*) labor force statistics for ever-married one-parity women twenty to twenty-four years of age who have children under the age of three. The NLS labor force participation rate for all such women is 42.9 percent, compared with 34.5 percent for the decennial census. Of the 8.4 percentage point difference, 5.4 percent are in the employed part time, with a job but did not work, and unemployed categories. For black women, all of the difference in rates (an NLS labor force participation rate of 62.9 percent compared with a census rate of 52.7 percent) can be attributed to these three categories.

On the basis of this information, several rationales for the differences in the rate levels are suggested: (1) our analysis excludes a small number of women enrolled in school who have lower levels of work attachment; (2) all of the NLS interviews are with the respondent herself who may be more likely to recall marginal work activities than would another household member—in the decennial census and the Current Population Survey other household members sometimes respond for the woman herself; and finally, (3) over the years, an NLS respondent may acquire a "sensitivity" to the standard labor force series of questions asked. Given the respondent's awareness of the major objective of the NLS interviews, she may make a greater effort to recall work activities of a marginal nature.

7. It should be emphasized that causation in most of this analysis is not implied to be in only one direction. While we frequently seem to imply causation in much of what we write, we wish to reiterate that the interrelationships among the work, fertility, and other socioeconomic variables—adding in the dimension of time—are far more complex than can be handled within space and time constraints of this chapter.

8. Implicit in this discussion is the assumption that there are high correlations between fertility expectations and prospective fertility behavior. While we cannot obviously answer this question regarding the long run, we have some evidence that the association does indeed hold in the short run. Between 1971 and 1973, 51 percent of the one-parity white women who expected three or more children had an additional child compared with 36 percent for those who expected a total of two children and 14 percent for those who expected only one. Similar but less pronounced patterns were evidenced among the black one-parity women.

9. For studies that offer useful and perhaps analogous situations focusing on Jewish-Americans and Americans from rural backgrounds integrating into the larger society, see Sidney Goldstein and Calvin Goldscheider, *Jewish Americans* (Englewood Cliffs, N.J.: Prentice-Hall, 1968), or David Goldberg, "The Fertility of Two Generation Urbanites," *Population Studies* (March 1959):214-222. Several mobility and reference concepts are intertwined in our research. Upward mobility conscious individuals may restrict fertility for economic motives—that is, they may try to improve their own economic status to an acceptable level in an absolute sense, as well as to improve their economic status relative to relevant peers. From a psychological perspective, these individuals may be striving to acquire characteristics more in tune with their perceived notions of what their peers view as proper behavior. In a loose sense, Robert K. Merton in *Social Theory and Social Structure* (New York: The Free Press, 1968) defines these latter two relative concepts within a relative deprivation and anticipatory socialization framework.

10. To simplify the empirical analysis, our universe is restricted to young women who are not in school. Hence, we will not consider schooling further at this time.

11. Evidence of an inverse relationship between other family income and wife's labor force participation, demonstrating a negative effect on wife's labor supply, is common in the literature on labor force participation. For example, see William G. Bowen and T. Aldrich Finegan, *The Economics of Labor Force Participation* (Princeton, N.J.: Princeton University Press, 1969). Ideally, one would like to use a measure of "permanent" rather than current income. However, data limitations force us to use current income.

12. More formally, we are hypothesizing that the substitution effect of the woman's (potential) wage will outweigh the income effect.

13. For example, see Bowen and Finegan, *The Economics of Labor Force Participation*. Such a positive relationship could also result from a positive partial correlation (that is, controlling for wage) between education and the nonpecuniary aspects of work.

14. See C. Russell Hill and Frank P. Stafford, "Allocation of Time to Preschool Children and Educational Opportunity," *Journal of Human Resources* 9 (Summer 1974):323-341; and Arleen Leibowitz, "Education and Home Production," *American Economic Review* 64 (May 1974):243-250. This may reflect not simply a "taste" phenomenon, but rather an independent effect of education on productivity in the home (and particularly on child care).

15. In addition to the income, wage, and taste variables, we have included several other variables in the analysis. These variables are included primarily as controls designed to prevent biased estimation of our hypothesized relationships, and consist of:

1. A self-evaluative measure of the respondent's health status. We assume that respondents whose health limits the amount or kind of work they can do in the labor market will be less likely to be in the labor force.

2. A dichotomous variable indicating whether or not there is another adult (age twenty-one or over and exclusive of the respondent's husband) in the household. This variable is included only for the periods after the birth. Since another adult in the household provides a *relatively* good substitute for the mother's time at home, we hypothesize that, other things being equal, respondents from such households will have higher labor force participation rates.

3. A categorical variable differentiating women who are married with spouse present from other women (widowed, divorced, separated, married with spouse absent, and never married). Clearly, even after controlling for the other variables in the model, it is likely that marital status will influence labor force participation, since women of different marital statuses have quite different long-term prospects. We hypothesize that, other things being equal, married women living with their husbands will have lower participation rates than other women.

16. Note, however, that the discussion in this section of the potential wage rate as a measure of the opportunity cost of nonmarket time suggests that, to the extent that black women have lower wage rates than white women, children will be less expensive (in terms of foregone income) for them.

17. Note that there are some women who do not drop out of the labor force except for very brief periods of time.

18. One should keep in mind, however, that we are in no sense focusing here on a rare event. As already demonstrated in this chapter, substantial proportions of women, *particularly* blacks, return to work soon after the birth of their first child.

19. For evidence on this point, see Steven H. Sandell and David Shapiro, "The Theory of Human Capital and the Earnings of Women: A Re-examination of the Evidence," *Journal of Human Resources* 13 (Winter 1978).

# Appendix 3A:
# Defining the Universe
# and Selected Variables

## Universe Descriptions

In the analysis of labor force participation rates before the first birth, a respondent is not selected for any cross-sectional universe unless her first child was born between the 1968 and 1973 interview dates. Each model requires a scan of all survey dates (1968 to 1973) to select women in the appropriate time interval relative to the child's birth. As a result of this procedure, any one respondent may be represented in more than one model. Information for the explanatory variables is drawn from the survey at which the respondent reaches the required time period for each model. As an additional universe restriction, no respondent can be enrolled in school at the survey date referenced.

Respondents selected for the change in wage models must have been employed before and after the birth of their first child. The reference point for each explanatory variable is either implicit in the variable title or explained in the variable definition.

## Dependent Variables

In the analysis of labor force participation rates surrounding the first birth, there are a total of five dependent variables, each associated with one of five cross-sectional models. An individual who is in the labor force during the indicated time interval receives a value of 1 on the dependent variable, otherwise she receives a value of 0. The five selected time intervals are divided as follows: (1) eighteen to thirteen months prior to the birth of the first child; (2) twelve to six months before; (3) five to zero months before; (4) one to five months after the birth; and (5) six to twelve months after.

For the analysis of changes in wage before and after the first birth, the dependent measure is created by dividing the hourly rate of pay on the first postbirth job by the hourly rate of pay on the last prebirth job, and multiplying the resulting quantity by 100.

## Estimating Potential Wage

Separate wage equations were estimated for white and black working women. Wages were expressed in 1967 dollars. For whites the wage equation was as follows (with $t$ statistics in parentheses):

$$\text{Wage} = \underset{(2.99)}{143.38} - \underset{(-2.80)}{20.802 \times (\text{Education})} + \underset{(5.64)}{1.6313 \times (\text{Education}^2)}$$

$$+ \underset{(9.25)}{20.357 \times (\text{Work experience})} - \underset{(-4.47)}{0.97405 \times (\text{Work experience}^2)}$$

$$+ \underset{(5.01)}{24.725 \times (\text{SMSA})} - \underset{(-1.25)}{6.4141 \times (\text{South})}$$

Number of observations = 1,482          $R^2$ (adjusted) = .26

The wage equation for blacks (with $t$ statistics in parentheses) was:

$$\text{Wage} = \underset{(3.59)}{186.22} - \underset{(-2.33)}{19.717 \times (\text{Education})} + \underset{(4.05)}{1.4391 \times (\text{Education}^2)}$$

$$+ \underset{(6.89)}{17.022 \times (\text{Work experience})} - \underset{(-5.20)}{1.2564 \times (\text{Work experience}^2)}$$

$$+ \underset{(3.35)}{20.748 \times (\text{SMSA})} - \underset{(-7.28)}{40.068 \times (\text{South})}$$

Number of observations = 523          $R^2$ (adjusted) = .33

The potential wage variable was created by using the coefficients of the preceding equations in conjunction with the characteristics of each respondent (that is, education, work experience, etc.) to impute a potential wage rate for each respondent, regardless of whether she was currently in the labor force.

# 4

## Sex Segregation in the Labor Market: An Analysis of Young College Women's Occupational Preferences

*Patricia K. Brito* and
*Carol L. Jusenius*

Over the past several years there has been a growing interest in occupational patterns of female employment. Evidence of this is the expanding literature on the concentration of women in a relatively small number of occupations and on the extent to which they are moving out of these "stereotypically female" occupations into ones that have been characterized as "stereotypically male."[1] Concurrently, there has been much concern about the effects on women of changing demands for workers in specific occupations. For example, the projected oversupply of individuals training to become teachers has significant ramifications for college-educated women.[2]

This chapter explores both these areas. In the first major section we analyze the characteristics of college-educated or college-bound young women who stated a desire to be in occupations typically held by men. In the second major section we examine the extent to which these women's aspirations regarding employment in specific occupations have changed between 1968 and 1973 and the relationship between the shifts and projected demand. In both sections our sample is restricted to young women who state that they plan to be working outside the home at age thirty-five.

### Occupational Preference: Typical vs. Atypical Occupations

Occupational segregation of women in the American labor market has been a persistent phenomenon. According to the 1940 decennial census, 63 percent of all women in the labor force were in occupational categories in which 50 percent or more of the incumbents were female. By 1970, the comparable percentage was about 65 percent.[3]

### *The Importance of Occupational Segregation*

Research has found that occupational segregation has had a profound effect on wages. Workers of both sexes who are in predominantly female occupations earn

57

substantially less than similarly educated persons in characteristically male occupations.[4]

Given that workers in typically female occupations are at an economic disadvantage relative to their counterparts in typically male occupations, it is not clear why women enter these occupations. Proponents of affirmative action programs have argued that demand-side factors—that is, the preference of employers for men or women in certain occupations—are to a large extent responsible for existing occupational segregation. However, when young women who expect to be working at age thirty-five are asked in what occupation they would *like* to be, the vast majority mention occupations typically held by women. For example, in 1973, among young women in college or anticipating a college education, 78 percent of the blacks and 75 percent of the whites indicated they expected to hold a stereotypically female occupation. Hence, it seems probable that the predominance of women in certain occupations reflects, in part, their own preferences. Stated another way, it appears that supply-side factors are also responsible for occupational segregation.

To the extent that women prefer a typically female occupation, affirmative action programs directed solely at employers will not substantially reduce occupational segregation. Hence, in addition to pursuing a vigorous affirmative action program, public policy undoubtedly should be concerned with counseling and educational programs if young women are to be informed about the full range of available occupations.

If the observed preferences of women for a relatively small number of occupations do reflect their tastes for particular kinds of work, this suggests that stereotypically female occupations may have characteristics that correspond especially well to women's requirements. For example, job opportunities in these occupations may permit geographic mobility; hours of work may be flexible; or there may be little financial penalty associated with leaving and subsequently reentering the labor force.

An alternative, but not mutually exclusive, explanation is that the choice of a typically female occupation is the product of the socialization process within the family and society or of the policies of educational institutions. To some extent, the personal attributes of a young woman should reflect her past social or educational experiences. To the degree that these determine the strength of her labor market commitment and her views on those occupations which are suitable for women, one would expect the probability of choosing a stereotypically masculine career to vary by the personal characteristics of the respondent.

In this chapter we attempt to identify the personal characteristics of women that are correlated with the choice of a typically male occupation. By limiting our analysis in this fashion, we do not deal with the characteristics of the occupations themselves that might make them especially attractive or convenient for women. Nevertheless, identification of those attributes of young women which influence their preferences for typically male or female occupations is important: it provides information necessary for the formulation of public policy aimed at reducing supply-side barriers to entry into typically male occupations.

Clearly there are a myriad of factors associated with both the individual and specific types of work that influence a woman's choice of occupation. In selecting among them, we have chosen to focus on those suggested by previous research in the area of women's occupational preferences.

## Previous Research

Previous research on this subject can be roughly characterized as reflecting two schools of thought. One group of studies, found chiefly in the vocational and psychological counseling literature, has suggested that the concentration of women in a relatively small number of occupations reflects the differentiated sex roles found within the family and society. For instance, a mother's role as "homemaker" and a father's role as "income earner" may act as signaling devices to the daughter regarding her expected role as an adult. Familial roles that provide a woman with a broader view of her "proper" sphere will also tend to increase the probability of her entering a less traditional occupation.[5] A second argument has been that family size and the sex distribution of the children are factors that influence a young woman's occupational choice. For a given level of income, the smaller the number of children, the greater the amount of resources that can be devoted to each child. Furthermore, if a young woman is an only child or if there are no sons in the household, all the parents' ambitions will be centered on the daughter(s). Thus in small families, there is a higher probability that daughters will receive the financial aid and encouragement necessary for those atypical, professional occupations that require extensive training.[6]

Another group of researchers, notably human capital theorists, have suggested that women's concentration in a select number of occupations may arise from a rational economic motive. These economists argue that, when earnings *over the life cycle* are considered, incumbents of typically female occupations may *not* be at an economic disadvantage relative to their counterparts in typically male occupations. That is, if typically female occupations are characterized by a relatively high initial wage and a relatively flat lifetime earnings profile, it may be economically rational for women to enter these occupations if they expect a short working career.[7] In contrast, men, who typically foresee a long working career, tend to invest in themselves by entering occupations that may have a lower initial wage but higher future earnings. Women who also expect a sufficiently long working career would behave in a manner similar to their male counterparts: they would be willing to sacrifice present wages to maximize wages over the long run. Hence, these women would be interested in the same types of occupations as men and would be likely to choose an occupation in which men predominate.

## The Empirical Model

The model of occupational choice presented in this chapter refines both the human capital and the vocational counseling perspectives of occupational preference. First, it includes in one empirical model both those variables describing aspects of the childhood familial environment suggested by the literature in vocational counseling and those measures of career commitment suggested by the human capital school. In addition, it is assumed that while the roles played by one's parents are important determinants of occupational choice, their effect may be modified by later schooling and work experience. Hence, the model includes variables measuring certain aspects of previous educational and labor market experiences.

Specifically, the model explores the correlates of the expectation of being in a typically male occupation at age thirty-five as reported by young women who anticipate being in the labor force at that age. Thus we deal with plans outlined in 1973, for a time that is from six to sixteen years in the future.[8] The sample is further restricted to young women who in 1973 were in college, had completed one or more years of college and were no longer enrolled, or reported they expected to attend college. Results are reported separately for blacks and whites. The sample was stratified by race because of the possibility that black and white women live in different social contexts or may well be affected in different ways by the same social milieus.[9]

The technique employed in this investigation is Multiple Classification Analysis (MCA). With MCA we can determine for each category of every independent variable that proportion of women which anticipated a male occupation at age thirty-five, assuming that members of the category are "average" in terms of all other variables included. Differences in these proportions among the several categories of a variable are interpreted as indicating the "pure" association of that variable with the probability of a young woman's choosing an atypical occupation.

The dependent variable is dichotomous with the value of 1 if the woman aspired to a typically male occupation, and 0 if her choice was a typically female occupation. (For simplicity, those occupations which are stereotypically male will be referred to as "atypical," those which are stereotypically female, as "typical.") Typical occupations are defined empirically as those in which the percentage of incumbents who are women exceeds the percentage of women represented in the total experienced civilian labor force. Since women were 38.1 percent of the experienced civilian labor force in 1970, typical occupations are those in which 38.2 percent or more of the incumbents in 1970 were women. In an analogous fashion, atypical occupations are those in which 38.1 percent or less of the workers were women in 1970. By this definition, about 75 percent of the women in the experienced civilian labor force at the time of the 1970 census would have been classified as being in a typical occupation.[10]

*Empirical Results*

For ease of exposition, the total set of independent variables has been divided into three major categories: Familial Environment, Educational and Labor Market Experience, and Potential Labor Market Involvement. The results are reported in tables 4-1 and 4-2 for white and black women, respectively.[11]

*Familial Environment*

This set of variables corresponds most closely to those which have been studied as determinants of occupational choice in the vocational counseling and psychology literature. Here we hypothesized first that those women whose mothers were highly educated or had worked outside the home would have an above average probability of choosing an atypical occupation.

The empirical results indicate that the relationship between the mother's experiences and the daughter's occupational expectations differ by race. A variable representing the mother's education and type of occupation had a statistically significant influence only on white young women. However, the patterns of significance were not consistent with the role model hypotheses. Of the women who had lived with their mothers, only two groups had an above average probability of preferring an atypical occupation: those whose mothers only had a high-school education and had worked in a *typical* occupation, and those whose mothers had at least some college education, but were *not working* when the daughter was fourteen years of age.

This finding does not necessarily imply that mothers have no influence on white women's occupational choices. White women who lived in households headed by their mothers had a higher than average likelihood of expecting to be in an atypical occupation.

Our hypothesis that small family size would be positively associated with the expectation of an atypical occupation is supported by the data. Specifically, among white women, those without siblings had a higher than average probability of aspiring to an atypical occupation. Among blacks, those with two or fewer siblings in the family showed a higher than average probability of choosing a typically male occupation.

*Educational and Labor Market Experience*

Clearly, the influence of a family on a young woman's career aspirations may be modified by her educational and labor market experience. For college students, the sex composition of the student body where a woman attends college might be expected to affect her occupational aspirations. One argument advanced in

**Table 4-1**

**Unadjusted and Adjusted Percentages of White College Women Choosing an Atypical Occupation by Selected Characteristics of Familial Environment, Experience, and Potential Labor Market Involvement: Multiple Classification Analysis**

| Selected Characteristics | Number of Respondents | Unadjusted Percent | Adjusted Percent |
|---|---|---|---|
| *Familial environment* | | | |
| Mother's education and type of occupation[a] | | | ** |
| 0 to 12 years school and: | | | |
| Worked at atypical occupation | 44 | 11.7 | 11.4 |
| Worked at typical occupation | 193 | 28.5 | 28.7 |
| Did not work | 347 | 20.9 | 23.1 |
| 13 to 18 years school and: | | | |
| Worked at atypical occupation | 19 | b | b |
| Worked at typical occupation | 83 | 26.8 | 20.9 |
| Did not work | 131 | 28.4 | 26.3 |
| Did not live with mother | 22 | b | b |
| Not ascertainable or occupation not reported | 38 | 45.2 | 41.2 |
| Occupation of male head of household[a] | | | ** |
| Professional, technical or managerial | 352 | 26.1 | 25.6 |
| Other | 431 | 22.0 | 22.4 |
| Lived with mother only | 63 | 37.6 | 39.8 |
| Not ascertainable or occupation not reported | 31 | 28.5 | 23.7 |
| Number of siblings | | | ** |
| None | 66 | 31.9 | 31.1 |
| One or more | 805 | 24.1 | 24.1 |
| Not ascertainable | 6 | b | b |
| Birthplace of parents | | | ** |
| One or both parents born in Latin America, Central, Southern, or Eastern Europe | 47 | 38.1 | 33.0 |
| Neither parent born in Latin America, Central, Southern or Eastern Europe | 818 | 27.7 | 24.9 |
| Did not live with either parent | 11 | b | b |
| Not ascertainable | 1 | b | b |
| *Educational and labor market experience* | | | |
| Educational level and sex composition of college student body | | | ** |
| Not yet in college in 1972 | 218 | 19.2 | 20.5 |
| In college by 1972 and student body composition is: | | | |
| Less than 31 percent female | 66 | 33.0 | 33.4 |
| 31 to 60 percent female | 457 | 27.8 | 26.0 |
| More than 60 percent female | 69 | 33.5 | 33.0 |
| Nursing schools | 29 | 2.5 | 11.7 |
| Not ascertainable | 38 | 16.6 | 21.5 |

**Table 4-1** (cont.)

| Selected Characteristics | Number of Respondents | Unadjusted Percent | Adjusted Percent |
|---|---|---|---|
| Age in 1973 | | | *** |
| 19 to 22 | 337 | 25.1 | 22.7 |
| 23 to 25 | 281 | 21.0 | 21.4 |
| 26 to 29 | 259 | 28.8 | 31.7 |
| Number and type of occupations, 1968 to 1973[c] | | | *** |
| No work experience | 28 | 3.8 | 13.1 |
| 1 or 2 different occupations and: | | | |
| Worked in an atypical occupation | 28 | 32.6 | 34.2 |
| Other | 208 | 13.4 | 14.5 |
| 3 or 4 different occupations and: | | | |
| Worked in an atypical occupation | 103 | 31.4 | 30.4 |
| Other | 196 | 22.9 | 21.7 |
| 5 or 6 different occupations and: | | | |
| Worked in an atypical occupation | 103 | 32.6 | 30.3 |
| Other | 82 | 30.3 | 31.4 |
| 7 or more different occupations | 79 | 36.0 | 34.9 |
| Not ascertainable | 50 | 34.1 | 34.4 |
| *Potential labor market involvement* | | | |
| Number of times reported expectation of working at age 35[c] | | | * |
| 1 | 57 | 16.3 | 16.5 |
| 2 | 114 | 16.3 | 21.2 |
| 3 | 124 | 33.7 | 33.1 |
| 4 | 148 | 27.9 | 26.9 |
| 5 | 204 | 22.7 | 22.7 |
| 6 | 217 | 26.5 | 24.5 |
| Not ascertainable | 13 | b | b |
| Marital status | | | * |
| Married, spouse present | 495 | 22.2 | 25.6 |
| Separated, divorced, widowed or married—spouse absent | 58 | 34.7 | 35.9 |
| Never married | 324 | 27.3 | 22.2 |
| Childbearing expectations and number of children | | | *** |
| No children in household and: | | | |
| No more children expected | 78 | 40.9 | 39.0 |
| More children expected | 450 | 26.6 | 27.0 |
| 1 child in household and: | | | |
| No more children expected | 42 | 41.4 | 38.4 |
| More children expected | 129 | 16.2 | 17.3 |
| 2 children in household and: | | | |
| No more children expected | 83 | 15.5 | 16.3 |
| More children expected | 38 | 11.2 | 7.0 |
| 3 or more children in household | 41 | 8.0 | 8.0 |

**Table 4-1** (cont.)

| Selected Characteristics | Number of Respondents | Unadjusted Percent | Adjusted Percent |
|---|---|---|---|
| Not ascertainable | 16 | b | b |
| Grand mean | 877 | 24.9 | 24.9 |
| $R^2$ (adjusted) | | | .109*** |

[a]Refers to time when respondent was fourteen years of age.
[b]Percentages not shown where base represents less than twenty-five respondents.
[c]Further information on these characteristics is available from the authors.
*Significant at the 10 percent level.
**Significant at the 5 percent level.
***Significant at the 1 percent level.

favor of female colleges has been that women in such an environment are less influenced by a stereotyping of sex roles that would discourage them from majoring in traditionally male-dominated fields, such as the pure sciences or mathematics, or from assuming leadership positions. However, offsetting this is the probability that predominantly male or mixed colleges are more likely to offer the curriculum necessary to enter an atypical occupation. Given these two opposing effects, one cannot hypothesize the direction of the relationship between the sex composition of the college attended and the sex label of the expected occupation.

The empirical results indicate that sex composition of the college attended was indeed related to the choice of an atypical occupation for both whites and blacks. However, only among white women was attendance at either a predominantly men's or women's college associated with an above average probability of aspiring to an atypical occupation. For blacks, attending a female college was correlated with a *lower* probability of choosing an atypical occupation; attending a mixed college was associated with a *higher* probability.

Of course, the direction of causation cannot be inferred with certainty. Young women who attend male colleges may, *even before entering*, be relatively unconstrained by sex stereotypes and comfortable in social or work situations where men are a majority. Furthermore, the choice of a predominantly male or mixed college may have been the result of a *previous* occupational decision that required a curriculum not available at a female college. In a similar vein, young women who attend female colleges may, *prior to entrance*, believe that attendance at such a college is important because of the "constraining" influence introduced by the presence of men in more mixed institutions.[12]

In addition to educational experiences, the number and types of occupations a young woman has held may serve to broaden the range of occupations that she considers potentially desirable to enter. Previous research has indicated that the greater the number of different occupations a young woman has held, the higher the likelihood that she will be interested in entering an atypical occupation in the future.[13] In this model we have included a variable that not only represents previous experience in a variety of occupations, but also represents (for white women) previous experience in atypical occupations specifically.[14]

For white women, this measure of exposure to the labor market proved to be a powerful influence on the likelihood of expecting to enter a male occupation. Those women who had prior experience in atypical occupations had a higher than average probability of expecting to be in an atypical occupation in the future. Moreover, the greater the number of occupations previously held, the higher the probability of choosing an atypical occupation.

In contrast, among black college women, although the number of occupations previously held was related to occupational expectations, this relationship was not monotonic. Furthermore, when a measure of both the number and the type of past occupations analogous to that used in the white college women's model was included in the black college women's equation, it proved to be insignificant.

*Potential Labor Market Involvement*

To estimate the relationship between commitment to the labor market and the expectation of holding a typically male occupation at age thirty-five, several variables were employed. One is a direct measure of the women's beliefs regarding their own future labor force involvement. Two other variables—marital status and present and expected family size—also capture the likelihood that the women will participate extensively in the labor force.

The direct measure of a woman's commitment to employment is a variable that represents the consistency in all six interviews of the respondent's expectation to be working at age thirty-five. This variable proved to be insignificant.

Results of the variable reflecting number of children currently in the household and childbearing expectations are particularly interesting. As expected, white women who had either no children or only one child and who expected no additional children had a higher than average probability of choosing an atypical occupation for age thirty-five. Furthermore, regardless of the current family size, those who anticipated no additional children were also more likely to expect to be in a male occupation than those women who anticipated having additional children.

However, among black college women, family size did not appear to

**Table 4-2**
**Unadjusted and Adjusted Percentages of Black College Women Choosing an Atypical Occupation by Selected Characteristics of Familial Environment, Experience, and Potential Labor Market Involvement: Multiple Classification Analysis**

| Selected Characteristics | Number of Respondents | Unadjusted Percent | Adjusted Percent |
|---|---|---|---|
| *Familial environment* | | | |
| Family composition[a] | | | ** |
| Lived with mother and father and: | | | |
| Mother worked | 120 | 21.7 | 22.0 |
| Mother did not work | 102 | 17.9 | 15.1 |
| Lived with mother only and: | | | |
| Mother worked | 56 | 17.5 | 17.6 |
| Mother did not work | 12 | b | b |
| Other | 49 | 32.0 | 34.6 |
| Education of head of household[a] | | | |
| Less than high school | 200 | 18.5 | 20.8 |
| High school | 56 | 27.0 | 24.1 |
| More than high school | 27 | 35.8 | 29.0 |
| Not ascertainable | 56 | 21.0 | 19.1 |
| Number of siblings | | | ** |
| 2 or fewer | 89 | 33.9 | 32.5 |
| 3 or 4 | 93 | 18.2 | 17.7 |
| 5 or more | 155 | 17.1 | 18.1 |
| Not ascertainable | 2 | b | b |
| *Educational and labor market experience* | | | |
| Educational level and sex composition of college student body | | | ** |
| Not yet in college in 1972 | 144 | 15.0 | 16.3 |
| In college by 1972 and student body composition is: | | | |
| Less than 61 percent female | 139 | 28.3 | 28.2 |
| More than 60 percent female | 38 | 20.8 | 15.5 |
| Not ascertainable or nursing schools | 18 | b | b |
| Age in 1973 | | | |
| 19 to 22 | 174 | 26.1 | 25.9 |
| 23 to 25 | 78 | 22.2 | 19.3 |
| 26 to 29 | 87 | 14.3 | 16.6 |
| Number of occupations held, 1968 to 1973[c] | | | ** |
| No work experience | 10 | b | b |
| 1 or 2 different occupations | 81 | 14.6 | 15.1 |
| 3 different occupations | 63 | 29.4 | 26.0 |
| 4 different occupations | 68 | 16.7 | 16.5 |
| 5 different occupations | 58 | 31.9 | 35.2 |
| 6 or more different occupations | 45 | 22.6 | 23.2 |
| Not ascertainable | 14 | b | b |

**Table 4-2** (cont.)

| Selected Characteristics | Number of Respondents | Unadjusted Percent | Adjusted Percent |
|---|---|---|---|
| *Potential labor market involvement* | | | |
| Number of times reported expectation of working at age 35[c] | | | ** |
| 1 or 2 | 24 | b | b |
| 3 or 4 | 64 | 25.0 | 25.7 |
| 5 or 6 | 249 | 21.5 | 21.1 |
| Not ascertainable | 2 | b | b |
| Marital status | | | |
| Married, spouse present | 133 | 16.1 | 18.2 |
| Separated, divorced, widowed, or married–spouse absent | 40 | 20.7 | 25.3 |
| Never married | 166 | 27.7 | 24.5 |
| Childbearing expectations and number of children | | | |
| No more children expected and: | | | |
| Fewer than 2 children in household | 46 | 12.9 | 13.9 |
| 2 or more children in household | 54 | 15.5 | 19.0 |
| More children expected and: | | | |
| No children in household | 149 | 27.8 | 24.7 |
| 1 child in household | 57 | 18.5 | 18.8 |
| 2 or more children in household | 28 | 25.5 | 31.7 |
| Not ascertainable | 5 | b | b |
| Grand mean | 339 | 21.9 | 21.9 |
| $R^2$ (adjusted) | | | .073*** |

[a]Refers to time when respondent was fourteen years of age.
[b]Percentages not shown where base represents less than twenty-five respondents.
[c]Further information on these characteristics is available from the authors.
 **Significant at the 5 percent level.
***Significant at the 1 percent level.

influence occupational choice. This suggests that, unlike their white counterparts, black women do not perceive a trade-off between time commitments to a family and time commitments to the labor force.

Marital status had little or no relationship to occupational aspirations among either racial group. Thus it appears that the presence of children (only among white women) and not marriage per se has a negative effect on the probability of selecting a typically male occupation.

*Comparison of Racial Groups*

The empirical models presented in the previous section indicate that the determinants of expectations regarding employment in a typically male or a typically female occupation vary between the racial groups. No one factor or set of factors appears to be systematically related to the occupational aspirations of all women. Hence, one implication of these results is that demographic changes—such as smaller family sizes—will not be similarly associated with occupational choice for black and white college women. A second implication of our findings is that, if occupational integration is a social goal, then policies formulated to affect supply-side factors must take into consideration racial differences among women.

The racial variations in factors influencing occupational expectations are not surprising. The two groups may well have lived in different social and familial environments when they were young. It is also likely that some of the variations are attributable to historical patterns of occupational segregation by race. Historically, the number and types of occupations open to black college-educated women may differ from those open to their white counterparts. Hence, while the dependent variable may have accurately categorized occupations that are typical and atypical for white women, it may be a less accurate measure of occupations that are typical or atypical for black women.[15]

Finally, the results indicate that a young woman's family background is, at best, only weakly associated with occupational choice. Although the data available give a very incomplete indication of the childhood environment of the women, the findings suggest that one need not be "deterministic" about the possibilities for increasing occupational integration. A young woman's choice between a typical or an atypical occupation is not determined solely by her childhood environment; educational and labor market experiences later in life also have an important impact.[16]

## Occupational Preferences and Occupational Outlook

In assessing the probable success of these women in finding work in their preferred fields, it is useful to examine the growth prospects of the occupations that were frequently mentioned as desired occupations for age thirty-five. Clearly, young women who are planning careers in fields that are growing slowly and where competition is keen may be frustrated in achieving their career goals, even with the requisite education and training. Among such women who drop out of the labor force, subsequent reentry may require retraining or education for another career.

*Occupational Preferences*

Table 4-3 shows the specific occupations mentioned in 1968 and 1973 by young women who expect to be working at age thirty-five.[17] These data suggest that if young women are able to realize their occupational ambitions for age thirty-five, they will still be concentrated in a relatively small number of occupations. Among both white and black women who have attended or plan to attend college, approximately 60 percent want employment in only three general areas: teaching, health services, and clerical work.

Table 4-3 also shows, among specific *atypical* occupations, the distributions of respondents who expect to be in stereotypically male occupations at age thirty-five. These data show rather dramatically that the range of occupational choice is very narrow, even among those young women who plan to enter atypical occupations. Of the more than 200 stereotypically male occupations, only 16 were mentioned by the women in either 1968 or 1973. Moreover, in 1973 only three respondents expected to be engineers; one, a pilot; and four, architects.

On a more positive note, interest was evinced in several occupations that had not been listed by five or more women in 1968. For example, in 1973, of the black women who expected to be working in an atypical occupation at age thirty-five, 6 percent indicated they expected to be members of the police force, and 5 percent indicated they expected to be accountants.

*Occupational Projections*

Occupational projections suggest that many of the fields in which women have traditionally been a majority will have a high or moderate growth rate. As table 4-4 indicates, most occupations in the health field are expected to have excellent growth prospects. Similarly, rapid growth for workers in clerical occupations was forecast in 1973. Secretaries in particular were projected to have excellent chances for employment throughout the 1970s and early 1980s.

On the other hand, there is an expected decrease in the number of openings for teachers. In 1968, 1973, and 1974, the Department of Labor consistently projected that teaching at both the primary and secondary levels would, at best, be a very slow growth occupation. Table 4-3 indicates a concurrent decline in the percentage of our sample who expect to be teachers. In 1968, 47 percent of the whites who planned to go to college and expected to be employed at age thirty-five planned a teaching career. In 1973, this percentage had dropped by 16 percentage points. However, even with such a decline in the percentage of women planning teaching careers, 31 percent of the whites and 23 percent of the

**Table 4-3**

**Occupational Expectations for Age Thirty-five of Women Expecting or Attending College as Reported in 1968 and 1973 by Race[a]**

*(Percentage Distributions)*

| | 1968 | | 1973 | |
|---|---|---|---|---|
| *Occupational Expectation* | *Whites* | *Blacks* | *Whites* | *Blacks* |
| **All occupations** | | | | |
| Number of respondents | 448 | 279 | 877 | 339 |
| Total percent | 100 | 100 | 100 | 100 |
| Teachers | 47 | 35 | 31 | 23 |
| Health workers | 14 | 22 | 19 | 22 |
| Registered nurses, technicians | 10 | 12 | 15 | 16 |
| Practical nurses, attendants | 1 | 4 | 2 | 5 |
| Physicians, pharmacists | 3 | 7 | 1 | 2 |
| Clerical | 8 | 25 | 13 | 15 |
| Secretaries | 6 | 18 | 6 | 8 |
| Social workers | 3 | 5 | 5 | 5 |
| Psychologists | 1 | 1 | 2 | 1 |
| Lawyers | 2 | 0 | 1 | 1 |
| Hairdressers | 1 | 1 | 1 | 3 |
| Accountants | 1 | 0 | 2 | 1 |
| Managers | 2 | 1 | 3 | 3 |
| All others | 22 | 9 | 24 | 25 |
| **Atypical occupations** | | | | |
| Number of respondents | 102 | 39 | 220 | 72 |
| Total percent | 100 | 100 | 100 | 100 |
| Accountants | b | b | 9 | 5 |
| Authors | 5 | 2 | 3 | 3 |
| College and university professors | 9 | 0 | 10 | 5 |
| Designers | 6 | 3 | 2 | 6 |
| Lawyers and judges | 7 | 2 | 4 | 3 |
| Physicians | 14 | 44 | 5 | 8 |
| Psychologists | 4 | 5 | 8 | 6 |
| Sports instructors | 6 | 12 | 5 | 2 |
| Technicians, other engineering and physical sciences | 4 | 2 | b | b |
| Veterinarians | 7 | 0 | b | b |
| Professional, technical and kindred workers[c] | 7 | 6 | 12 | 23 |
| Farmers and farm managers | b | b | 3 | 0 |
| Managers, officials and proprietors[c] | 8 | 10 | 13 | 14 |
| Real estate agents | b | b | 4 | 1 |
| Operatives[c] | b | b | 1 | 2 |
| Police | b | b | 2 | 6 |
| All others | 24 | 15 | 20 | 17 |

[a]Sample size in 1968 differs from that in 1973 because each constitutes an independent cross section of the respondents. The universe for each year consists of black and white women who answered in that year that they planned to be working at age thirty-five and named the occupation at which they expected to work.

[b]Percentages calculated only for those occupations that five or more respondents mentioned as their occupational choice for age thirty-five at the relevant interview date. Those mentioned by fewer than five persons are included in the "all others" category.

[c]Not elsewhere classified.

blacks were still planning to teach in 1973. Clearly, there are lags in the adjustment to the poor occupational outlook for teachers, and the oversupply of teachers will probably continue.

Those occupations for college graduates that are expected to have excellent employment opportunities, for the most part, were not mentioned significantly more often by the 1973 sample than by the 1968 sample. For example, the percentage expecting to be employed as social workers, psychologists, or accountants was not significantly higher in 1973 than in 1968. The one possible exception is a slight increase in the percentage of white college women who foresaw working in the health field. This increase is largely the result of the more frequent choice of work as a registered nurse.

Of the atypical professions mentioned, several—for example, accountants, physicians, and veterinarians—were projected in 1973 to be rapidly expanding. Unfortunately, however, the proportion of young women expecting to work as physicians or veterinarians declined between 1968 and 1973. Also, a larger percentage of women indicated a desire to be in some fields, such as management or college teaching, that should have only moderate or slow increases.[18]

In general, in spite of the broad range of atypical occupations that could have been mentioned, the occupational expectations of young women who anticipated being in a stereotypically male occupation were limited. Unfortunately, too, the demand for several of the occupations mentioned is expected to be below average.

### Summary and Conclusions

This chapter has analyzed the factors associated with a young college woman's expectation of being in an occupation at age thirty-five that is atypical for women. It has been found that the factors affecting expectations vary by race. For example, the presence or expectation of children negatively affects the likelihood that white college women will expect to be in a male occupation, but it has no significant effect on black college women.

The chapter has also shown that the number and types of occupations to which women aspire, regardless of their sex typing, is limited. Moreover, although extensive publicity has been accorded women who have become truck drivers and telephone-line repair workers (for example), and even though there is a broad range of stereotypically male occupations from which young women might choose, they actually tend to mention relatively few occupations.

Thus it is clear that if young women are to move into all types of typically male occupations, affirmative action programs are not sufficient. It is also necessary to increase young women's awareness of both the full range of their employment opportunities and the growth prospects of the occupations of their choice.

**Table 4-4**

**Occupational Projections for Occupations Expected at Age Thirty-five by Year in which Projection Was Made**

| 1968-1969[a] | 1972-1973[a] | 1974[a] |
|---|---|---|
| *High Growth*[b] | | |
| Health professions: | Health professions: | Health professions: |
|   Registered nurses |   Registered nurses |   Registered nurses |
|   Health technologists |   Health technologists |   Health technologists |
|   and technicians |   and technicians |   and technicians |
|   Practical nurses |   Practical nurses |   Practical nurses |
|   Health aides, except |   Health aides, except |   Health aides, except |
|   nurses (nurses aides, |   nurses (nurses aides, |   nurses (nurses aides, |
|   orderlies) |   orderlies) |   orderlies) |
| ●Physicians | ●Physicians | ●Physicians |
| ●Veterinarians | ●Veterinarians | ●Veterinarians[d] |
| ●Psychologists[e] | ●Psychologists[e] | ●Psychologists[e] |
| Social workers | Social workers | ●Lawyers |
| ●Engineering and science | ●Engineering and science | Social workers |
| technicians | technicians | ●Engineering and science |
| ●College and university | ●Accountants | technicians |
| teachers[e] | Hairdressers | ●Police and detectives |
| ●Accountants | Secretaries | ●Professional and |
| Stenographers | Clerical workers (all) | technical workers[f] |
| Hairdressers | | Secretaries |
| | | Clerical workers (all) |
| *Moderate Growth*[c] | | |
| ●Lawyers | ●Lawyers | ●Accountants |
| ●Pharmacists | ●Pharmacists | ●Pharmacists |
| ●Managerial occupations | ●Managerial occupations | ●Managerial occupations |
| ●Police and detectives | ●Police and detectives | ●Designers |
| ●Designers | ●Designers | ●Real estate agents and |
| ●Real estate agents and | ●Real estate agents and | brokers |
| brokers | brokers | ●Writing professions |
| ●Writing professions | ●Writing professions | Hairdressers |
| Clerical workers (all) | ●College and university | |
| | teachers[e] | |
| *Slow Growth*[d] | | |
| Prekindergarten teachers | Prekindergarten teachers | Prekindergarten teachers |
| Elementary school | Elementary school | Elementary school |
| teachers | teachers | teachers |
| High school teachers | High school teachers | High school teachers |
| ●Farmers and farm | ●Farmers and farm | ●Farmers and farm |
| managers | managers | managers |
| ●Operatives (all) | ●Operatives (all) | ●Operatives (all) |
| | | ●College and university |
| | | teachers[e] |

Sources: U.S. Department of Labor, Bureau of Labor Statistics, *Occupational Outlook Handbook*, 1968-69; 1972-73; and 1974-75. Max L. Carey, "Revised Occupational Projections to 1985," *Monthly Labor Review* (November 1976):10-22.

[a]Projections for 1968-1969 usually concern the period until the mid-1970's. The projections for 1972-1973 extend to the end of the decade; those for 1974 are for 1974 to 1985.

**Table 4-4** (cont.)

bIncludes occupations in which employment is expected to increase by 30.0 percent or more with job opportunities "excellent" or "very good."
cIncludes occupations in which employment is expected to increase between 15.0 and 29.9 percent with job opportunities "good or favorable."
dIncludes occupations in which employment is expected to increase not more than 14.9 percent (may also experience decline) with job opportunities "competitive."
eWith Ph.D. only.
fNot elsewhere classified.
•Atypical occupation for women.

## Notes

1. For example, see Valarie Kincaid Oppenheimer, "The Sex-Labeling of Jobs," *Industrial Relations* 7 (May 1973):219-234; Carol L. Jusenius and Richard L. Shortlidge, Jr., *Dual Careers: A Longitudinal Study of the Labor Market Experience of Women*, vol. III, Manpower Research Monograph no. 21, U.S. Department of Labor (Washington, D.C.: U.S. Government Printing Office, 1975); and Victor Fuchs, "A Note on Sex Segregation in Professional Occupations," *Explorations in Economic Research* 2 (Winter 1975):105-111.

2. For example, see The Carnegie Commission on Higher Education, *College Graduates and Jobs* (New York: McGraw-Hill, 1973).

3. The 1970 estimate is based on figures for the experienced civilian labor force from the U.S. Bureau of the Census, Census of the Population: 1970. *Subject Report* PC (2)-7A, *Occupational Characteristics* (Washington, D.C.: U.S. Government Printing Office, 1973). The 1970 occupational categories were coded into the 1960 classification scheme, which is more nearly comparable to that used in 1940. See John A. Priebe, Joan Heinkel, and Stanley Greene, *1970 Occupation and Industry Classification Systems in Terms of Their 1960 Occupation and Industry Elements*, U.S. Bureau of the Census Technical Paper no. 26 (Washington, D.C.: U.S. Government Printing Office, 1972).

4. Donald J. Treiman and Kermit Terrell, "Women, Work, and Wages—Trends in the Female Occupation Structure" in *Social Indicator Models*, eds. Kenneth C. Land and Seymour Spilerman (New York: Russell Sage Foundation, 1975), pp. 157-199. Also see Carol L. Jusenius, "The Influence of Work Experience and Typicality of Occupational Assignment on Women's Earnings" in Herbert S. Parnes et al., *Dual Careers: A Longitudinal Analysis of the Labor Market Experience of Women*, vol. IV, Manpower Research Monograph no. 21, U.S. Department of Labor (Washington, D.C.: U.S. Government Printing Office, 1976), pp. 97-118.

5. For examples, see Elizabeth M. Almquist and Shirley S. Angrist, "Role Model Influences on College Women's Career Aspirations," *Merrill-Palmer*

*Quarterly* 17 (July 1971):263-279; David L. Klemmack and John N. Edwards, "Women's Acquisition of Stereotyped Occupational Aspirations," *Sociology and Social Research* 57 (July 1973):510-525; and Donna L. Nagely, "Traditional and Pioneer Working Mothers," *Journal of Vocational Behavior* 1 (October 1971):331-341.

6. Anne Roe, *The Making of a Scientist* (New York: Dodd, Mead, 1953); and David L. Klemmack and John N. Edwards, "Women's Acquisition of Stereotyped Occupational Aspirations," *Sociology and Social Research* 57 (July 1973):510-525.

7. Harriet Zellner, "The Determinants of Occupational Segregation" in *Sex, Discrimination, and the Division of Labor*, ed. Cynthia Lloyd (New York: Columbia University Press, 1975), pp. 125-143; Barry Chiswick, James Fachler, June O'Neill, and Solomon Polachek, "The Effect of Occupation on Race and Sex Differences in Hourly Earnings," *Public Data Use* 3 (April 1975):2-9; and Solomon Polachek, "Occupational Segregation: An Alternative Hypothesis," *Journal of Contemporary Business* 5 (Winter 1976):1-12.

8. We believe that by studying expectations, we have a "purer" measure of occupational choice than is found in studies that examine a woman's presence in a particular occupation, since presence in an occupation is clearly determined by both demand conditions and personal preferences. Of course, the respondent may prefer an occupation simply because she feels job prospects are good in that field. However, it is felt that the question of what she would *like* to be doing at age thirty-five, by virtue of its being less related to present labor market conditions, is a better measure of preference.

9. Statistical analysis verified the need for this stratification.

10. To define typical and atypical occupations, 1970 classifications were converted into their 1960 equivalents using Priebe, Heinkel, and Greene, *1970 Occupational and Industry Classification*, since occupations in the National Longitudinal Surveys' (NLS) data are reported in their 1960 codes. Other definitions 5 and 10 percentage points above or below the 38.1 percent reference point were tested in preliminary analysis. Since the results did not differ significantly among the three definitions, only the results of the one model are presented here.

11. White women had a slightly higher proportion expecting to be in atypical occupations at age thirty-five than black women—25 and 22 percent, respectively. It will be apparent to the reader that the empirical models reported here differ between the racial groups. While the same model was run for both groups, only the best results are reported here. Where a comparison of identical models is useful, the results are mentioned in the text.

12. A hypothesis regarding the relationship between years of schooling and the typicality of the expected occupation could not be tested. Given the age of our sample in 1973 (nineteen to twenty-nine), many respondents were still attending college. Therefore, highest grade completed would not necessarily

represent the level of schooling the respondents would attain. A further argument against the use of highest grade completed for the college universe is that attendance in graduate school is probably the *result* rather than the cause of choosing an atypical career.

13. See Lenore W. Harmon, "Anatomy of Career Commitment in Women," *Journal of Counseling Psychology* 17 (1970):77-80; Almquist and Angrist, "Role Model Influences"; and Elizabeth Almquist, "Sex Stereotypes in Occupational Choice: The Case of College Women," *Journal of Vocational Behavior* 5 (August 1974):13-21.

14. For the respondent to be coded as having held an atypical job, she must have been in an atypical occupation different from that anticipated for age thirty-five. This procedure was followed so that we would avoid using the *result* of an earlier decision to work in a typically male occupation as the *predictor* of a choice for the future.

15. Black women are underrepresented in some typically female occupations and overrepresented in others. For example, while black women were 12 percent of the female labor force in the 1970 census, they comprised only 3 percent of the female secretaries and 8 percent of the female nurses (U.S. Bureau of the Census, *Occupational Characteristics*).

16. Of course, we cannot discard the possibility that these later experiences are associated with factors in the childhood environment that we do not measure. For example, certain women may be predisposed because of attitudes learned in childhood to acquire experience in atypical occupations or to work at a greater number of occupations.

17. Related occupations are grouped together. For example, the category "teachers" includes the following: elementary and secondary school teachers, sports instructors and officials, musicians and music teachers, dancers and dancing teachers, and artists and art teachers.

18. Some of the decrease in women expecting to be physicians or veterinarians is probably the result of a readjustment of expectations that were initially unrealistic.

# 5

# Work Attachment, Investments in Human Capital, and the Earnings of Young Women

*David Shapiro* and
*Timothy J. Carr*

This chapter examines the determinants of average hourly earnings of young women. The primary objective of the chapter is to analyze the impact of work expectations on investments in human capital and on hourly earnings, with particular focus on postschool investments in human capital. In addition, a comparable analysis will be made for young men to examine differences in the wage structures by sex and the underlying sources of the wage gap between young men and young women.[1]

## Postschool Investments in Human Capital

According to the human capital model of the distribution of earnings,[2] investments in human capital, such as schooling and on-the-job training, enhance a worker's productivity and, hence, earnings. Considerable empirical evidence has consistently documented the theoretically expected association between wages and accumulated human capital. Recently, the process of investment in human capital by women over the life cycle has been subjected to considerable theoretical and empirical analysis.[3] In considering investments in human capital over the life cycle, a very important difference between women and men emerges. Women often drop out of the labor force for extended periods of time, while the labor force participation of men, particularly married men, is consistently very high. The intermittent labor force participation of women is closely associated with the bearing and raising of children.[4]

The pattern of labor force participation of women, particularly married women, has two important implications for their human capital investment behavior. First, since women will spend less time over the life cycle engaged in work in the labor market, they will have less time to acquire on-the-job training than men of comparable age and schooling, and employers may also be more reluctant to provide such training. Second, returns in the form of higher wage rates to investments in human capital can only be received while the individual is at work. Hence, prospective discontinuity in lifetime labor force experience will

The authors wish to thank Leyla V. Woods for her research assistance.

77

have the effect of lowering the returns from, and consequently lowering the incentive for investments in on-the-job training.[5]

The preceding paragraph focuses on implications of the life-cycle human capital model with regard to sex differences in on-the-job training. However, the model also has implications regarding differences in investment behavior among women. To the extent that there are substantial differences in lifetime labor force attachment among women, the human capital model implies that women with stronger labor force attachment will engage in postschool human capital investments more heavily than women with weaker labor force attachment. A further implication is that the timing of investments will also differ. Investment profiles for women with greater commitment to work should be more similar to the monotonically declining investment profiles of men than those for women with weaker commitment to work.

Thus in examining wage rates and human capital investments of young women and men, we may distinguish *three* groups: (1) women whose expected attachment to the labor force over the life cycle is weak; (2) women whose expected attachment is (relatively) strong; and (3) men, whose expected attachment is strongest. According to human capital theory, investments in on-the-job training[6] should be increasingly important as one moves across these groups. Differences in postschool investment behavior between the first two groups and differences in investment between the second and third groups will be examined separately.

**Wage Equations for Young Women**

In this section, wage structures of "weakly committed" and "strongly committed" young women are estimated. The primary focus here is on whether these empirical estimates are consistent with our hypothesis that investments in on-the-job training are greater for women with strong attachment to the labor force.

*Specification*

The basic equation to be estimated is

$$\ln \text{Wage} = \alpha_0 + \alpha_1 \text{School} + \alpha_2 \text{Exper} + \alpha_3 \text{Tenure} + \sum_{i=1}^{6} \alpha_{4i} Z_i$$

where ln Wage is the natural logarithm of the respondent's hourly wage rate; School measures the highest grade of school completed; Exper measures the total number of years the respondent worked six months or more since she last attended school full time; Tenure measures the number of years that the respondent has held her current job; and $Z_i$ represents a set of control variables: a continuous variable measuring ability (IQ) and separate dummy variables for (1) workers whose wages are set by collective bargaining, (2) those who reside in the South, (3) those who reside in an SMSA, (4) those who work in the public sector, and (5) those who have work-limiting health problems.[7]

The semilogarithmic specification of the wage equation guarantees that the predicted hourly rate of pay generated by the model will always take on a positive value. It also means that the coefficients may be interpreted as the percentage effects on the wage rate of unit changes in the independent variables—that is, completing an additional year of schooling, ceteris paribus, will result in an increase in the hourly wage rate of $100 \times \alpha_1$ percent.

The first three independent variables in the equation—schooling, total work experience, and current job tenure—are human capital variables, and their coefficients are expected to be positive. Total experience and job tenure represent periods during which postschool human capital investments will be made. Holding tenure on current job constant, the coefficient of total experience measures the return to general training, while the coefficient of tenure in this specification measures the return to firm-specific training.[8]

The life-cycle human capital model is implicitly concerned with investment in general training. Hence, in the context of the wage equations to be estimated here, the hypothesis that postschool investments will be greater among women with stronger expected lifetime labor force attachment may be seen as implying that the coefficient $(\alpha_2)$ of total experience will be greater among such women than among women with weaker labor force attachment.

Behaviorally, postschool investments in general human capital will be manifested largely through occupational choice. Occupations differ in the amount of on-the-job training required to reach full effectiveness. Human capital theory suggests that "high-training" occupations will be characterized by low wages in the initial phase of experience (while the worker is acquiring the necessary skills through on-the-job training) and increasing wages as experience and the individual's capabilities to perform the job increase. Consequently, experience-wage profiles will be steep for "high-training" occupations and relatively flat for "low-training" occupations. Presumably, women with stronger expected lifetime labor force attachment will have greater incentive to invest in their general human capital by choosing "high-training" occupations. This greater investment, in turn, should be reflected in steeper experience-wage profiles—that is, a larger coefficient of total experience and a lower intercept term $(\alpha_0)$.

Apart from the influence of schooling, total work experience, and tenure, several control variables representing additional determinants of wage rates are included in the wage equations. Ability, measured here by an intelligence quotient (IQ) score, has been shown to be an important independent factor influencing wages.[9] Since our empirical focus is on the experience-earnings profiles implied by the experience coefficients in the wage equations, controlling for ability is imperative to ensure that the profiles are not simply reflecting ability differences between the strongly and weakly attached young women.

Considerable empirical evidence has been presented in the literature indicating that, other things being equal, wage rates are higher for workers whose wages are set by collective bargaining, who work in the public sector, and who reside in large urban areas. Similarly, wages tend to be lower, ceteris paribus, for workers who have health problems and who reside in the South.[10] Since the distributions of strongly and weakly attached women across these characteristics may differ, it is desirable to control explicitly for the effects of these factors. In brief, the control variables are introduced into the wage equations to prevent bias in the testing of our hypothesized relationships.

The array of variables just described exemplifies the advantages of using the National Longitudinal Surveys (NLS) relative to other microdata sources for the empirical analysis of wage determination. A comparison with the work of Mincer,[11] a typical example of the use of U.S. Census (1/1000 sample) data for this purpose, is most instructive. First, Mincer was forced by data limitations to use an annual earnings measure as a dependent variable. Such a variable varies with the amount of labor supplied as well as with human capital factors.[12] In this study we use a "purer" measure: an hourly rate of pay. Second, Mincer used a measure of potential experience obtained by the formula

$$\text{potential experience} = \text{age} - \text{highest grade completed} - 5.$$

This proxy is clearly untenable for samples (such as young women) characterized by less-than-continuous labor force participation.[13] Again, the NLS permit us to ascertain the *actual* labor market experience of our sample with tolerable accuracy.[14] Finally, we avail ourselves of information on "ability" (IQ), collective bargaining coverage, tenure on current job, and health status that is not generally available in the 1/1000 census sample or other microdata sets.

*Stratification*

Thus far, the discussion has focused on the distinction between women whose expected attachment to the labor force over the life cycle is weak and women whose expected attachment is strong. This distinction will be used to stratify the sample for purposes of estimating wage equations. The critical operational question is by what criterion will women be judged to be weakly or strongly committed to the labor force?

In this study we have made use of a woman's future plans as an indicator of the strength of her attachment to the labor force.[15] Respondents were asked in 1968 what they would like to be doing at age thirty-five. Presumably, those who stated that they would like to be working in the labor market are those with a greater attachment to the labor force, while those who expressed a preference for being housewives/mothers and those who responded "don't know" have weak attachment to the work force.

Those respondents in our sample who indicated a desire to work at age thirty-five differed very little in terms of their personal characteristics from those who did not indicate such a desire. For instance, the average white woman in the "plans" group was 24.6 years old, had 13.2 years of schooling, had worked 4.5 years since leaving school, and expected to bear 2.1 children. Her counterpart in the "no plans" group was 23.8 years old, had 13.1 years of schooling, 4.3 years of work experience, and anticipated 2.3 children. The "typical" black "plans" woman was 24.3 years old, had 12.6 years of schooling and 4.3 years of work experience, and expected to have 2.3 children. The corresponding figures for the black "no plans" group are 24.5 years, 12.8 years, 4.5 years, and 2.2 children, respectively. Thus, the future plans variable appears to be reasonably independent of these factors—that is, it is not serving simply as a proxy for some other (obvious) variable.

*Empirical Estimates*

In this section we focus on wage equations estimated for out-of-school women who were employed as wage and salary workers in 1973. The hypothesis of interest here is that women who desire to work at age thirty-five will invest more heavily in on-the-job training. Consequently, they will have steeper experience-wage profiles. In the context of the wage equation presented earlier, our hypothesis indicates that women who plan to work should have a larger coefficient for total work experience and a smaller intercept (constant) term.

The procedure used to test this hypothesis is as follows. For black and white women separately we have estimated wage equations in which interaction terms for total work experience, tenure, and the constant, are included to differentiate those who plan to work at age thirty-five. Within each equation, the interaction terms allow for differences between those who plan to work and those who do not plan to work in terms of the coefficients of total work experience, tenure, and the constant.[16]

The empirical results pertinent to our principal hypothesis are presented in table 5-1.[17] We estimated the wage equations using quadratic specifications for both total experience and tenure.[18] These quadratic specifications make comparison of the "plans" and "no plans" groups a bit more complex than in the case of a linear specification, since there are two coefficients for each of the two work experience measures. With a quadratic specification, the coefficient of

**Table 5-1**
**Regression Coefficients Relating ln Wage to Selected Variables by Race and Plans to Work at Age Thirty-five[a]**

| | Whites | | | Blacks | | |
|---|---|---|---|---|---|---|
| Variable[b] | Plan to Work | No Work Plans | Significance Level[c] | Plan to Work | No Work Plans | Significance Level[c] |
| Total work experience (years) | .0762 | .0335 | * | .0543 | .0424 | |
| Total work experience squared | −.0041 | −.0014 | | −.0052 | −.0039 | |
| Tenure on current job (years) | .0652 | .0831 | | .0470 | .0303 | |
| Tenure on current job squared | −.0041 | −.0064 | | d | d | |
| Constant | 3.5664 | 3.6720 | * | 3.6583 | 3.7340 | |
| Number of respondents | 264 | 706 | | 127 | 138 | |

[a]The sample consists of women who were employed as wage and salary workers and were not enrolled in school full time as of the 1973 survey, and for whom the required data are ascertainable.

[b]For the full model, see table 5-2.

[c]Significance level refers to whether the coefficients of a particular variable differ significantly according to plans to work.

[d]Not included in this equation.

*Significant at the 10 percent level.

the linear term measures the initial steepness of the relationship in question, while the coefficient of the squared term reflects the rate at which the steepness changes as the independent variable increases.

The coefficients in table 5-1 reveal that for both whites and blacks, the relationship between hourly wages and total work experience is initially steeper (significantly so for whites) for those who plan to work at age thirty-five as hypothesized. In addition, within each racial group, the intercept term is lower for the "plan to work" group (again, the difference is significant for whites). This evidence thus provides tentative support for the human capital hypothesis that women with stronger expected attachment to the labor force will invest more heavily in general on-the-job training. At the same time, however, the coefficients of the experience-squared terms indicate that the initially steeper experience-wage profiles for those who plan to work at thirty-five flatten out more rapidly than the profiles for those with no work plans, although the latter effect is not statistically significant.

Figure 5-1 shows that this flattening out is not very consequential for the range of total work experience relevant to our inquiry—that is, figure 5-1 shows

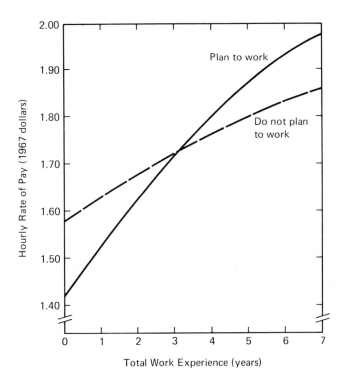

Note: Assumes twelve years of school, an IQ of 100, zero tenure, no health problems, residence in a non-Southern SMSA, and employment in a private sector job not covered by a collective bargaining agreement.

**Figure 5-1.** Experience Wage Profiles for Young White Women by Plans to Work at Age Thirty-five

experience-wage profiles for young white women according to whether they plan to be in the labor market at thirty-five. The profiles are drawn assuming twelve years of schooling, IQ of 100, zero tenure, residence in nonsouthern SMSA, wages not set by collective bargaining, employment in the private sector, and no health problems.[19] As implied by human capital theory, the profile for those women with stronger expected lifetime attachment to the labor force begins at a lower point and then rises more rapidly than the profile for weakly attached women, reflecting investment in training via reduced wages initially and returns to investment in the form of more rapid growth in wage rates subsequently. While the "plan to work" group's profile does flatten out somewhat more rapidly, it remains steeper than the profile for the "no work plans" group throughout the range of experience depicted in the figure.

Table 5-1 also reports differences by plans to work in the coefficients for tenure. Our principal hypothesis is concerned with investment in general training. However, interaction terms with tenure were included to see whether plans to work affect investment in specific training. In general, the evidence does not support the contention that women with stronger labor force attachment will invest more heavily in specific training. For example, within racial groups, there are no significant differences between the "plans" and "no plans" groups in the estimated tenure coefficients.[20]

In considering differences by race in the wage equations, it is apparent from table 5-1 that the plans/no plans distinction is more relevant for whites than for blacks. That is, the differences among blacks in the intercept and initial slope of the experience-wage profiles, while in the expected direction, are not significant and are smaller in magnitude than those for whites. Two possible reasons for such a phenomenon have been proposed.[21] First, greater labor market discrimination against black women than white women may prevent strongly attached black women from acquiring as much on-the-job training as they would like. In addition, minimum wage laws (which have a greater impact on blacks than whites) may have a similar effect. However, thorough examination of these and other hypotheses is beyond the scope of this chapter.

Comparison by race of the remaining coefficients in the wage equations reported in table 5-2 indicates that, with one exception, the coefficients are broadly similar. The exception is the coefficient for residence in the South. Among whites, a young woman who resides in the South is paid approximately 5 percent less, on average, than her nonsouthern counterpart, other things equal. Among blacks, the southern/nonsouthern differential exceeds 18 percent. It seems likely that this difference by race in the magnitude of the southern/nonsouthern wage differential is a reflection of greater labor market discrimination against blacks in the South.[22]

To summarize, there is empirical support here for the hypothesis that expected future labor force attachment will be an important determinant of accumulation of general human capital through investment in on-the-job training. It has been suggested elsewhere that young women tend to underestimate the likelihood of their being in the labor force after completing child raising.[23] Our results are consistent with the hypothesis that young women who do not anticipate future labor force attachment will not acquire much general training in job skills in the initial stages of their working lives. Consequently, it seems likely that many young women will be at a serious disadvantage if they attempt to reenter the labor force after raising a family. This suggests that young women should be more accurately apprised of the likelihood that they will be in the labor force following child raising, and the desirability of being adequately prepared for this labor market experience. Counseling and vocational guidance at both the secondary school and college levels could be utilized in this regard.

**Wage Differences by Sex and the Effects of
Postschool Investments in Training**

In the previous section, we found empirical evidence which supports the human capital hypothesis that postschool investments in general training are greater for young women with stronger expected attachment to the labor force over the life cycle. A further implication of human capital theory is that investments in training should be greater for young men than for young women, since women, but not men, usually face prospective discontinuity in lifetime labor force experience. This implication is considered in the present section, which examines differences in postschool investment behavior between the strongly attached young women and young men.[24]

In addition, for whites, we examine differences in the wage structures by sex more generally to inquire into the underlying sources of the wage gap between young men and young women—that is, the young women in our sample have a mean hourly rate of pay of $2.32, compared with $3.86 for men. Furthermore, 35.9 percent of the young men fall into the higher paying occupational categories (professional, technical, managerial, and craft workers), whereas a mere 25.0 percent of the young women hold such jobs. Despite these disparities, the female and male samples are quite similar in terms of personal characteristics. For instance, the young women are, on average, 23.3 years old and have 13.2 years of schooling. The corresponding figures for young men are 23.8 years and 13.0 years, respectively. It is true that the young men have more work experience than the young women (4.6 versus 3.4 years), but that is at least partly due to the fact that the variables are defined somewhat differently.

As noted previously, the comparative analysis of the wage rates of young women and young men is based on the 1972 survey of young women conducted between January and April 1972, and the 1971 survey of young men conducted between October 1971 and February 1972. Wage equations were estimated for both groups. The samples are comparable to those used in the analysis in the previous section in that they consist of persons who were not full-time students and who were employed as wage and salary workers at the time of the survey. The samples were further restricted to respondents who ranged in age from nineteen to twenty-eight.[25]

*Empirical Estimates*

The wage equations for young women who plan to work at thirty-five and for young men are reported in full in table 5-3. The specifications used generally followed those used in the previous section.[26] To illustrate the differing postschool general investment behavior of young men and strongly attached

**Table 5-2**
**1973 Wage Equations for Young Women by Race: Regression Results[a]**

| Independent Variable | Whites | | Blacks | |
|---|---|---|---|---|
| | Coefficient | t value | Coefficient | t value |
| Highest grade completed | .0790 | (10.73)*** | .0833 | (7.17)*** |
| Total work experience (years) | .0335 | (1.91)** | .0424 | (1.40)* |
| Total work experience squared | −.0014 | (−.86) | −.0039 | (−1.45)* |
| Tenure on current job (years) | .0831 | (4.64)*** | .0303 | (2.21)** |
| Tenure on current job squared | −.0064 | (−2.89)*** | b | b |
| Collective bargaining coverage | .1672 | (5.69)*** | .1659 | (4.54)*** |
| Public sector employment | .0433 | (1.45)* | .0136 | (.34) |
| Health problems | −.0561 | (−1.19) | .0848 | (.99) |
| Resident in SMSA | .1506 | (6.36)*** | .1702 | (3.78)*** |
| Residence in South | −.0451 | (−1.80)** | −.1811 | (−5.18)*** |
| Intelligence quotient | .0029 | (3.06)*** | .0032 | (2.49)*** |
| Desire to work at age 35 | −.1057 | (−1.43)* | −.0757 | (−.90) |
| Desire-work experience interaction | .0426 | (1.30)* | .0119 | (.29) |
| Desire-work experience squared interaction | −.0027 | (−.94) | −.0013 | (−.36) |
| Desire-tenure interaction | −.0179 | (−.57) | .0168 | (.84) |
| Desire-tenure squared interaction | .0023 | (.64) | b | b |
| Constant | 3.6720 | (30.61)*** | 3.7340 | (20.65)*** |
| $R^2$ (adjusted) | .331 | | .492 | |
| F ratio | 30.97*** | | 19.24*** | |
| Number of respondents | 970 | | 265 | |

[a]The sample consists of women who were employed as wage and salary workers and were not enrolled in school full time as of the 1973 survey, and for whom the required data are ascertainable. The dependent variable is the natural logarithm of the hourly rate of pay on the job held at the time of the 1973 survey (in 1967 dollars).
[b]Not included in this equation.
*Significant at the 10 percent level.
**Significant at the 5 percent level.
***Significant at the 1 percent level.

young women, we consider a "typical" young man and young woman, each of whom is a high school graduate who lives in a nonsouthern SMSA, has an IQ of 100, is employed in an establishment in the private sector not covered by a

**Table 5-3**
**Wage Equations by Sex: Regression Results[a]**

| Independent Variable | Young Women | | Young Men | |
|---|---|---|---|---|
| | Coefficient | t value | Coefficient | t value |
| Highest grade completed | .0474 | (2.99)*** | .0468 | (9.13)*** |
| Total work experience (years) | .0740 | (2.50)*** | b | b |
| Total work experience squared | −.0032 | (−1.07) | b | b |
| Potential work experience (years) | b | b | .0510 | (4.19)*** |
| Potential work experience squared | b | b | −.0020 | (−2.03)** |
| Tenure on current job (years) | .0383 | (1.16) | .0795 | (7.79)*** |
| Tenure on current job squared | −.0032 | (−.77) | −.0053 | (−4.81)*** |
| Collective bargaining coverage | .3068 | (4.94)*** | .2162 | (9.65)*** |
| Public sector employment | .1127 | (1.86)** | −.0623 | (−2.02)** |
| Residence in SMSA | .1496 | (2.95)*** | .1555 | (7.27)*** |
| Residence in South | .0394 | (.72) | −.0524 | (−2.26)** |
| Intelligence quotient | .0056 | (2.78)*** | .0036 | (4.23)*** |
| Constant | 3.6608 | (14.88)*** | 4.2565 | (39.88)*** |
| $R^2$ (adjusted) | .289 | | .282 | |
| F ratio | 12.92*** | | 49.77*** | |
| Number of respondents | 294 | | 1,241 | |

[a]The samples consist of white young women (men) who were employed as wage and salary workers and were not full time students as of the 1972 (1971) survey, and for whom the required data are ascertainable. The dependent variable is the natural logarithm of the hourly rate of pay on the job held at the time of the survey (in 1967 dollars).
[b]Not included in this equation.
**Significant at the 5 percent level.
***Significant at the 1 percent level.

collective bargaining agreement, and is new to the job (that is, has no tenure). The respective experience-wage profiles for two such hypothetical persons that are implied by the wage equations in table 5-3 are depicted in figure 5-2.

The profiles depicted in figure 5-2 do not offer very much support for the thesis that the male profile should start at a lower level and advance more rapidly than the profile for the young woman. For one thing, the man's profile lies uniformly above the woman's profile, despite the fact that it should be depressed at low levels of work experience. Another problem is that the two profiles are nearly parallel, diverging significantly only at high (eight years or

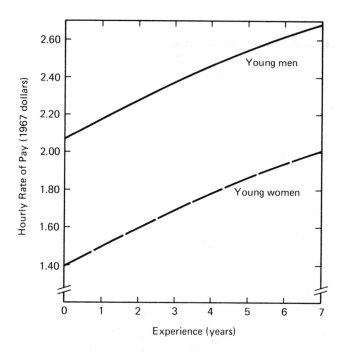

Note: Assumes twelve years of schooling, an IQ of 100, zero tenure, residence in a non-Southern SMSA, and employment in a private sector job not covered by a collective bargaining agreement.

**Figure 5-2.** Experience-Wage Profiles for a White "Strongly Attached" Young Woman and Young Man

more) levels of experience. Investigation of the sources of the gap between the two profiles (such as discrimination), apart from differential investment behavior, is an important topic which lies beyond the scope of this inquiry.

*Wage-Gap Analysis*

The technique of "wage-gap analysis" has been used by some researchers[27] to decompose the difference in average wages between two groups (for example, males and females, blacks and whites) into that portion which is accounted for by differential "endowments" of characteristics that are presumed to determine wages, and that portion which is accounted for by differences in the wage "structure." These portions are represented by the regression coefficients of estimated wage equations for the two groups in question. For example, blacks may earn less than whites partly because, on average, they have less schooling. Also, part of the actual gap may be due to a higher return per year of schooling for whites than for blacks. The former portion stems from different endowments, while the latter is a consequence of different wage structures.

In applying this technique to our samples of young women and young men, we first note that the geometric mean wage for the female sample is $2.06, whereas that for the male sample is $2.93.[28] If the young women had the average characteristics of the young men rather than their own characteristics, but were still subject to the female wage structure, the resulting geometric mean wage would be $2.15. Hence, using the female wage structure, the sex difference in endowments of those characteristics presumed to influence wages accounts for only $0.09 of the $0.87 difference in mean wages. Conversely, if the young men had the average characteristics of the young women, but were still subject to the male wage structure, the resulting geometric mean wage would be $2.76. Using the male wage structure, the sex difference in endowments accounts for $0.17 of the actual wage gap.[29]

Clearly, different endowments of these characteristics play only a minor role in determination of the wage gap among young workers. On the average, the different endowments of young men and women can account for only a little more than 15 percent of the wage gap. The remainder of the wage gap—that portion attributable to differences in the wage structure—may be viewed as an upper limit estimate of the impact of discrimination.[30]

**Summary and Conclusions**

We began by considering the role of expectations of future labor force attachment in influencing postschool human capital investment behavior. Three groups were distinguished: (1) women whose expected attachment to the labor force over the life cycle is weak; (2) women whose expected attachment is (relatively) strong; and (3) men, whose expected attachment is strongest. We hypothesized that investment in on-the-job training should increase as one moves across these groups.

Differences in postschool investment behavior between the weakly and strongly attached women were considered first. Human capital theory suggests that experience-wage profiles for workers who invest relatively heavily in on-the-job training will start at a lower point and be steeper in slope than those for workers with low levels of investment. Estimation of experience-wage profiles for the two groups of women provided tentative support for our hypothesis. The profiles for the strongly attached women began at a lower point and were more steeply sloped than those for the weakly attached women, suggesting that women in the former group do indeed invest more heavily in on-the-job training than women in the latter group. These differences in profiles were more pronounced among whites than among blacks.

We next examined differences among whites in postschool investment behavior between the strongly attached young women and young men. Estimation of experience-wage profiles for these two groups did *not* provide support for our hypothesis. We expected the profile for men to start at a lower point and be more steeply sloped. However, the estimated profiles for these two groups were essentially parallel, with the profile for women being considerably below that for men. In addition, a wage-gap analysis of the differences in wage rates between the young women and the young men revealed that sex differences in endowments of those characteristics presumed to determine wages could account for only a small portion of the average difference in wage rates. The remainder of the wage gap (that portion attributable to differences in the wage structure) may be viewed as an upper limit estimate of the impact of discrimination.

In brief, we find only partial support for our hypothesis that investments in on-the-job training will increase as one moves from weakly attached women to strongly attached women to men. The empirical evidence tentatively supports our hypothesis in comparing the two groups of women, but not in comparing the strongly attached women to the men.[31] This research raises important questions that deserve future examination. Why are differences in investment behavior between weakly attached women and strongly attached women more pronounced among whites than among blacks? Why are men paid considerably more than strongly attached women, despite the similar patterns of investment in on-the-job training for these two groups?

We have suggested that discrimination may be relevant in considering these questions. Rather than bringing in discrimination as a deus ex machina, however, future research should focus on attempting to clarify the impact of discrimination as well as other factors. For example, we noted earlier that postschool human capital investments will be manifested largely through occupational choice. The process of occupational choice and patterns of occupational mobility, and their relationships to expected lifetime labor force attachment and sex, are areas that deserve further study. Occupational choice and mobility are presumably influenced by labor market expectations, but they are also likely to be influenced by direct labor market discrimination and by social norms concerning the "proper" roles of women and men (indirect discrimination?). Greater understanding of the relative importance of each of these factors in determination of occupational attachment and wage rates would be most desirable.

## Notes

1. The initial analysis uses data from the 1973 survey of young women. However, since the 1973 survey of young men was a telephone survey and

consequently subject to considerable measurement error on several key variables, the comparative analysis between women and men makes use of the 1971 survey of young men and the 1972 survey of young women. These two surveys took place closer in time than did the 1971 surveys of young men and women.

2. For a discussion of this model, see Gary S. Becker, *Human Capital: A Theoretical and Empirical Analysis, with Special Reference to Education* (New York: Columbia University Press, 1964); Gary S. Becker, *Human Capital and the Personal Distribution of Income: An Analytic Approach*, Woytinsky Lecture no. 1 (Ann Arbor: University of Michigan, 1967); Jacob Mincer, "The Distribution of Labor Incomes: A Survey with Special Reference to the Human Capital Approach," *Journal of Economic Literature* (March 1970):1-26; and Jacob Mincer, *Schooling, Experience and Earnings* (New York: Columbia University Press, 1974).

3. For example, see Jacob Mincer and Solomon Polachek, "Family Investments in Human Capital: Earnings of Women," *Journal of Political Economy* (March/April 1974, Part II):S76-108; and Steven H. Sandell and David Shapiro, "The Theory of Human Capital and the Earnings of Women: A Re-examination of the Evidence," *Journal of Human Resources* (Winter 1978).

4. For evidence to this effect based on data from the 1967 NLS survey of mature women, see appendix A of Steven H. Sandell and David Shapiro, "The Theory of Human Capital and the Earnings of Women: A Re-examination of the Evidence," mimeographed (Columbus: The Ohio State University, Center for Human Resource Research, 1976). In view of the secular increase in female labor force participation, the reduction of fertility rates in recent years, and the evidence presented in chapter 3 herein, it seems most likely that time spent at home following the birth of the first child will be much shorter for the young women under consideration here than was the case for their older counterparts.

5. It has also been argued that prospective discontinuity of labor force experience affects the shape of the postschool investment profile of women—that is, while the investment profile for men is monotonically declining, the profile for married women with children is not. Rather, it tends to be higher in the postmaternal than in the prematernal period (Mincer and Polachek, "Family Investments in Human Capital"). However, as noted by Sandell and Shapiro in "The Theory of Human Capital," this hypothesis was not tested properly by Mincer and Polachek.

6. The term "on-the-job training" is used here in the broadest sense. It refers to any formal or informal process of learning skills that enhances productivity, and hence wages, while one is employed on a given job. This concept is discussed further later in this chapter.

7. Alternative specifications of the wage equation were also estimated. First, we explicitly included a variable identifying those individuals who had completed formal on-the-job training relevant to their current jobs. This variable was not statistically significant and it is not included in the regressions reported

here. Second, the regressions were estimated using quadratic specifications of the work experience variables. The quadratic specifications generally yielded a better fit, and are reported in the following pages. However, for illustrative purposes the discussion here focuses on the simple linear specification presented earlier.

8. This interpretation of the total experience and tenure coefficients is identical to that in Sandell and Shapiro, "The Theory of Human Capital." For a more rigorous theoretical justification of this interpretation, see David Shapiro, "Specific Human Capital, Job Tenure, and the Earnings of Women," mimeographed (Columbus: The Ohio State University, 1976). The concepts of general training and firm-specific training were first given prominent focus by Becker, *Human Capital*. Most simply, "perfectly general" training is training which raises a worker's productivity equally at many firms. Completely specific training raises a worker's productivity *only* with a single firm. Most types of real-world training involve both general and specific components. However, the mix of these components varies. For example, military training in electronics and a skilled-trades apprenticeship are two forms of predominantly general training. On the other hand, learning the rules and regulations in a particular firm and training as an astronaut constitute primarily specific training. For a more thorough discussion of these two types of training and the financing of training, see Becker, *Human Capital*.

9. See, for instance, John C. Hause, "Earnings Profile: Ability and Schooling," *Journal of Political Economy* 80 (May/June 1972, Part 2):S108-138.

10. A large number of studies provide evidence of wage differentials associated with one or more of these five factors. The interested reader may wish to consult Ronald Oaxaca, "Male-Female Wage Differentials in Urban Labor Markets," *International Economic Review* (October 1973):693-709, for a single study that considers all of these factors (as well as several others) simultaneously.

11. Jacob Mincer, *Schooling, Experience, and Earnings* (New York: Columbia University Press, 1974).

12. Alan S. Blinder, "On Dogmatism in Human Capital Theory," *Journal of Human Resources* (Winter 1976):8-22.

13. Ibid., 13-14.

14. A potential experience measure will be used in the case of young men examined later.

15. Other criteria that were tested included expected number of children and Specific Vocational Preparation (SVP) score of first postschool job (SVP score measures the time required to reach proficiency in a particular vocation). Insufficient variation in the former and reduced sample sizes associated with using the latter resulted in rejection of these criteria as stratification variables.

16. The coefficients for the "no work plans" groups are taken directly from the corresponding wage equations in table 5-1, while the coefficients for the

"plan to work" groups are obtained for each variable by summing the "no work plans" coefficient and the corresponding interaction term coefficient. For a further discussion of this and similar econometric procedures, see J. Johnston, *Econometric Methods*, 2nd ed. (New York: McGraw-Hill, 1972), pp. 176-186.

17. The interaction terms for tenure are included to see if investment in specific training is greater for women with stronger labor force attachment. An implicit assumption here is that the coefficients of the other variables in the wage equation do not differ by plans to work. A formal test indicated that this assumption is consistent with the data—that is, when interaction terms were introduced for all variables in the wage equation, there was no pattern of significant differences by plans to work in the coefficients of schooling or in any of the control variables.

18. One exception is in the specification of tenure in the equation for blacks. With the quadratic specification, both coefficients were insignificant and positive, presumably reflecting multicollinearity. Consequently, a linear specification of tenure was used for blacks. In any case, for both blacks and whites, the empirical differences by plans to work would be quite similar if we had reported estimates of the wage equations using linear specifications of total work experience and tenure.

19. Profiles generated from the wage equation depict the relationships between experience and the natural logarithm of the hourly wage rate. For purposes of figure 5-1, we have taken antilogarithms and drawn the figure with "wage" instead of "ln wage" on the vertical axis.

20. Among whites, the tenure-wage relationship is initially somewhat steeper for those women with no work plans, but flattens out more rapidly for these women as tenure increases. Table 5-1 indicates that among blacks, the tenure coefficient is greater for the women who plan to work at age thirty-five. However, this difference is not significant.

21. See Sherwin Rosen, "Learning and Experience in the Labor Market," *Journal of Human Resources* (Summer 1972):326-342.

22. For a discussion of regional differences in racial discrimination, see Gary S. Becker, *The Economics of Discrimination*, 2nd ed. (Chicago: University of Chicago Press, 1971).

23. According to Carol Jusenius and Steven H. Sandell, "Barriers to Entry and Re-entry into the Labor Force," (Columbus: Center for Human Resource Research, the Ohio State University, June 1974), in 1968, approximately 29 percent of the young white women in the NLS sample planned to work at age thirty-five. The corresponding figure for young black women was 59 percent. Actual labor force participation rates in 1967 for the older NLS women, thirty-three to thirty-seven years of age, were 47 percent for whites and 67 percent for blacks.

24. The overwhelming majority (over 85 percent) of strongly attached young women expect to bear children. Hence, on the average, young men should

have greater expected lifetime attachment to the labor force and greater incentive to invest in on-the-job training than the strongly attached young women.

25. If they had not been so restricted, the women would have ranged in age from eighteen to twenty-eight, and the men from nineteen to twenty-nine.

26. Information on health limitations was not available on the 1972 survey of young women. The variable representing health limitations was accordingly dropped from the men's equation to increase that equation's comparability to the young women's equation. Since information on actual work experience could not be ascertained for young men in the same way as for young women, potential work experience (time out of school) was used as a proxy.

27. For instance, see Alan S. Blinder, "Wage Discrimination: Reduced Form and Structural Estimates," *Journal of Human Resources* (Fall 1973):436-455; Andrew Kohen and Roger Roderick, "The Effects of Race and Sex Discrimination on Early-Career Earnings," mimeographed (Columbus: Center for Human Resource Research, The Ohio State University, 1975); and Oaxaca, "Male-Female Wage Differentials."

28. Due to the semilogarithmic specification of the wage equations, the use of the geometric mean hourly rate of pay (the antilogarithm of the mean of the natural logarithm of the wage) is more appropriate than the arithmetic mean.

29. The methodology used here involves the familiar index number problem. Hence, we get two estimates (establishing a range of possible values) of the importance of sex differences in endowments of those characteristics presumed to influence wages.

30. This analysis does not explore the question of whether the differences in endowments themselves are a result of discrimination; see Blinder, "Wage Discrimination."

31. In light of the evidence concerning brief labor force withdrawal associated with childbearing presented in chapter 3, one might argue that differences in lifetime labor force attachment between young men and "strongly attached" young women are negligible with regard to their impact on investments in on-the-job training. This view would account for the estimated profiles being nearly parallel. However, the difference in height remains unexplained.

# 6

# The Migration of Young Families: An Economic Perspective

*Steven H. Sandell* and
*Peter J. Koenig*

In this chapter the determinants of migration and the effect of migration on the labor market earnings of married men and women and single women are analyzed.[1] This study has relevance to policy considerations in at least two respects. First, to the degree that married women have their careers disrupted by the migration of their husbands or are inhibited from migrating to further their own careers, the effect of these factors must be taken into account when interpreting differences in wages between men and women with equal circumstances. Second, knowledge of the effect of unemployment on migration is a prerequisite to effective policies for dealing with the geographic dimension of structural unemployment.[2]

## The Theory of Family Migration

### The Model

In this development of a dual-location, work-leisure choice model, nonpecuniary benefits from working or living in either location are ignored.[3] The family is assumed to attempt to maximize its utility, which in turn is posited to depend on total family income, the wife's leisure, and the husband's leisure. Total family income is defined here to be a function of the wage rates of husband and wife and the amount of labor that each offers. The present model is an extension of the standard labor supply model in that the family is allowed to migrate, thereby changing the husband's and wife's wage rates. If the family does migrate, moving costs are subtracted from total family income.

The choice of residence depends not only on the wage rates obtainable by the husband and wife, but also on their dispositions to enter or remain in the labor market. A potentially high wage in a new location would *not* provide an incentive for the family to migrate if the wife would not choose to work at that wage. Hence, for families where the wife would not work at any conceivable wage, the decision to migrate becomes a function of only the husband's labor market opportunities. If the wife is willing to work at certain wage rates, then her labor market opportunities become a consideration in the family's location choice.

In families where the husband and wife both work we would expect less

95

migration than among other families—that is, the potential reduction in the wife's earnings is considered by the husband to be a cost of a geographic job change on his part and will constrain both his job search behavior and family migration. Similarly, it often does not pay for the wife to search for a job in a distant area until her husband has obtained satisfactory employment there.

The greater utility achieved in the new location for the migrant family can be associated with a change in its labor supply. Thus the new set of wage rates available to the migrant family can lead to (1) increased income with the same or an increased amount of leisure, (2) increased leisure at the same level of income, (3) increased leisure which more than compensates for reduced family income, or (4) increased family income which more than compensates for reduced leisure. It is also possible for the total family labor supply to remain relatively unchanged while the wife and husband change their individual hours of work in response to the new market wages.

As a consequence of migration, the family faces a new set of market prices on which it bases its behavior. Since there are costs to job switching and a job search often requires flexible hours, recent female migrants may refuse low-paying jobs (or jobs with little chance of career advancement) that will be immediately available in order to first make an extensive search of the new labor market. In addition, the high value the family places on the wife's time in setting up the new household may initially keep her out of the labor force. Hence, holding skill and education constant, we would expect to observe higher unemployment rates and lower labor force participation rates among married women who are recent migrants than among other married women.

Fertility plans, by affecting the costs associated with moving, can affect migratory behavior. If a working wife is planning to drop out of the labor force irrespective of the decision to move, the cost to the family of setting up a household in a new location will be reduced and, therefore, the likelihood of migration will be greater. On the other hand, the presence or prospect of a child may make the husband more cautious about quitting his job, thereby inhibiting migration. Conversely, migration may affect fertility plans. For example, the wife may decide to work fewer hours (or not at all) and revise her fertility plans if, as a result of migration, her wage rate is decreased or her husband's wage rate is increased.

*Unemployment, Unemployment Compensation, and the Propensity to Migrate*

In a two-worker family the unemployment status of each breadwinner is important. An employed person will migrate if job prospects appear better elsewhere. DaVanzo presents some empirical evidence showing that unemployed persons are more likely to migrate than are persons who are working.[4]

The receipt of unemployment compensation is expected to be negatively associated with migration. First, the receipt of compensation can reduce the pressure on the family to migrate. Second, to the extent that unemployment compensation subsidizes the job search only in the person's original area of residence (because of ignorance of the possibility of receiving compensation in another location), persons who receive unemployment compensation are less likely to migrate than are other unemployed persons.[5] In addition, job quitters are usually not eligible for unemployment compensation and are more likely to migrate.

The theoretical effect of national economic conditions on family migration is ambiguous. The greater number of employment opportunities during an economic upswing should induce more migration during prosperous than depressed economic periods. Also, it is well documented that job quits are lower when economic conditions are poor.[6] Risk-averse individuals will be less likely to make voluntary (geographic) job changes in poor as compared with prosperous times. On the other hand, since unemployed persons are more likely to migrate than employed persons, the migration rate could be greater during poor economic conditions when there are more unemployed.[7]

### The College Experience and the Propensity to Migrate

Aside from the effect of college on labor market earnings, other aspects of the college experience may contribute to later migratory behavior. In particular, living in a different city than that of one's parental family while attending college may be related to subsequent migration experience in the following manner. First, the decision to attend college out of town may reflect a "taste for migration." Persons who live away from their parents while in college probably originally have looser ties to their parents' residence than persons who attend college locally. If this is the case, these persons will be less likely to live in the locality in which they attended high school after they graduate from college.

In addition, even if those who attend college locally and those who go away to college begin college with similar "tastes for migration," the different college experiences may lead to different postcollege migratory behavior. To the extent that hometown ties are loosened during the college years for those who are away from home, these students are more likely to move to a new locale after graduation than are those who attend college in proximity to their high-school residence. Furthermore, local college attendees are more likely to find employment or to marry persons who have found employment in the local area.

### Family Income and the Migration Decision

In this section an economic model of the migration decision is presented which assumes that the family maximizes the present value of the sum of the future income streams of the husband and wife. If a family acts rationally and decides to move, it expects the present value of the returns to migration to exceed the cost of migration—that is, the expected lifetime earnings stream after migration must be greater than the expected earnings without migration by at least the cost of the move. For the household containing two persons who are willing to work, it is not possible to say anything about the income stream of either spouse separately without additional information. Maximization of family earnings implies that the sum of the two personal income streams must increase as a result of migration. This can happen if both increase *or* if the increase in the income stream of one spouse is greater than the reduction of the income stream of the other. The motivation for a family's migration could be due solely to improvement of the husband's earnings if the negative effect on the earnings of the wife is offset by the husband's improvement. Of course, the opposite could also hold true with the increase in the wife's earnings more than compensating for the decline in the husband's.

The model immediately yields a testable hypothesis: migrant families expect their total earnings stream after migration to be greater than it would have been without migration. Assuming that expectations are fulfilled (in the aggregate), and using earnings in a single year as a proxy for the earnings stream, the hypothesis can be tested with the National Longitudinal Surveys' (NLS) data. When relevant personal and labor market characteristics are controlled, it is hypothesized that the increase in labor market earnings of migrant families (between the year before and the year after migration) should be greater than the increase for nonmigrant families.[8] The relevant earnings figure for married women is the sum of their own plus their husbands' labor market earnings. For single women, only their own earnings are considered relevant.

**Empirical Tests**

In this section hypotheses developed from the model of family migration are tested empirically. These involve two aspects of migration: the determinants of migration and the effect of migration on family and individual earnings. Because of the limited number of observations for blacks, the empirical tests often focus exclusively on whites.

*The Likelihood of Migration*

The dependent variable to be used in the regression analyses is a dummy variable with the value of 1 if the family migrates, and the value of 0 otherwise.[9] A family is considered to have migrated if it reports that its county or Standard Metropolitan Statistical Area (SMSA) of residence is different in at least one of the survey years from 1969 to 1973 than it was in 1968.[10]

The probability of a family's moving depends on labor-market-related personal characteristics of each labor force participant. If migration is considered an investment, the incentive to move should decrease with age, since the length of time over which the person can reap benefits from moving decreases and the psychic costs of moving probably increase. Since the geographic scope of the labor market is likely to be larger for the highly educated than for the less educated, migration is expected to be positively related to education.[11]

For our purpose, however, these variables are control variables. Our chief interest is the effect of the wife's labor force commitment on the migration decision. Since it has been shown that a family is probably less likely to improve its economic position by migration if two persons rather than one are working, the propensity of the family to move is expected to be inversely related to the labor force commitment of the wife. Hence, variables for the wife's survey week employment status, job tenure, and weeks worked over the previous year will be introduced into three separate versions of the 1968 to 1973 family migration model.

To examine the effect of unemployment and unemployment compensation on migration, dummy variables are included in the regression analysis. These variables assume the value of 1 if the young woman was unemployed at the initial survey date or if she received any unemployment compensation during the previous year. Otherwise, the variables receive a value of 0. Since the interview schedules contain no direct question about the husband's unemployment experience, "husband's weeks worked over the previous year" is used as a proxy for his unemployment experience.

Attending college away from home is expected to be associated with greater postcollege migration. Thus a dummy variable equal to 1 if the wife attended a nonlocal college, and equal to 0 otherwise, is entered into the regressions. Finally, in addition to the 1968 to 1973 time span, identical regressions are run for the 1968 to 1970 and 1971 to 1973 time spans to ascertain if the propensity to migrate is influenced by the business cycle. Economic circumstances generally deteriorated over the six-year period. From 1968 to 1973 the annual unemployment rates were 3.6, 3.5, 4.9, 5.9, 5.6, and 4.9 percent, respectively.[12]

Table 6-1 summarizes the results of the determinants of migration. The coefficients indicate the percentage point change in the probability of migration per unit change in the independent variables (for an individual originally with the sample mean probability of migration).[13] As predicted, employment of the wife as measured by either the 1968 survey week employment status, weeks worked in 1967, or 1968 job tenure, were negatively related to the likelihood of migration between 1968 and 1973. For instance, if the wife is employed, the probability of family migration is 8 percentage points less than if the wife is not employed.[14] Also, in table 6-1, a married woman's nonlocal college attendance had a statistically significant positive effect on migration in all three samples, while local college attendance had an insignificant effect.[15]

The unemployment variables in table 6-1 have the expected effects on

**Table 6-1**

**Net Effects of Selected Variables on the Probability of Family Migration Between 1968 and 1973, 1968 and 1970, and 1971 and 1973: Logit Results[a]**

| Selected Variables | 1968-1973 Migration[b] | | | 1968-1970 Migration[c] | 1971-1973 Migration[d] |
|---|---|---|---|---|---|
| | (1) | (2) | (3) | | |
| Employed[e] | −.080** | | | .005 | .008 |
| Weeks worked in past year | | | −.005*** | | |
| Tenure[e] (in months) | | −.003*** | | | |
| Unemployed[e] | .013 | .019 | .009 | .067 | .137*** |
| Received unemployment compensation in past 12 months | −.200* | −.193* | −.190 | −.199* | −.168* |
| Attended nonlocal college | .123** | .142** | .125** | .113*** | .072 |
| Attended local college | .040 | .052 | .035 | −.003 | −.043 |
| Husband's weeks worked over past year | −.003* | −.004* | −.003* | −.003** | −.004*** |
| Husband received unemployment compensation in past 12 months | .024 | .018 | .047 | −.058 | −.108* |
| Husband's years of schooling completed | .013* | .015* | .015* | .001 | .018** |
| Husband's age | .004 | .005 | .007 | .002 | −.003 |
| Local area unemployment rate | −.0004 | −.0008 | −.0006 | −.0004 | .001 |
| Variance explained of model (Pseudo $R^2$)[f] | .05 | .06 | .08 | .04 | .09 |
| Chi-square of model | 19.0*** | 21.9*** | 27.8*** | 16.3*** | 28.5*** |

[a]The coefficients indicate the percentage point change in the probability of migration per unit change in the independent variables—that is, the coefficients equal $(B_i)(P)(1 - P)$, where the $B_i$'s are logit coefficients and $P$ is the sample mean probability of migration. All logit equations are based on unweighted data. Additional information on the original logit models is available from the authors.

[b]Universe consists of 528 white married respondents age seventeen to twenty-four in 1968. For all survey years (1968 to 1973), the following restrictions also apply: same spouse is present, neither respondent nor husband are enrolled in school, and husband of respondent is not in the military. The dependent variable is a dummy variable equal to 1 if respondent reports her SMSA or county of residence in 1969, 1970, 1971, 1972, or 1973 differs from her 1968 residence.

[c]Universe consists of 650 white married respondents age seventeen to twenty-four in 1968. For all survey years (1968 to 1970) the following restrictions also apply: same spouse is present, neither respondent nor husband are enrolled in school, and husband of respondent is not in the military. The dependent variable is a dummy variable equal to 1 if the respondent reports her 1968 SMSA or county of residence differs from her 1969 or 1970 residence.

[d]Universe consists of 534 white married respondents age seventeen to twenty-four in 1971. For all survey years (1971 to 1973) the following restrictions also apply: same spouse is present, neither respondent nor husband are enrolled in school, and husband of respondent is not in the military. The dependent variable is a dummy variable equal to 1 if the respondent reports her 1971 SMSA or county of residence differs from her 1972 or 1973 residence.

**Table 6-1** (cont.)

[e]At the 1968 (1971) interview date for the 1968 to 1970 and 1968 to 1973 equations
(1971 to 1973 equations).
[f]Pseudo $R^2 = [1 - \exp\{Z(L_w - L_r)/T\}]/[1 - \exp\{Z(L_w - L_{max})/T\}]$, where $L_w$ is the
maximum of the log of the likelihood function using a constant, $L_r$ is the maximum using
all variables, and $L_{max}$ is the maximum possible.
  *Logit coefficient significant at the 10 percent level.
  **Logit coefficient significant at the 5 percent level.
  ***Logit coefficient significant at the 1 percent level.

migration. Since the wife's unemployment and a smaller number of weeks worked by the husband are associated with a greater probability of migration, it seems that the labor market welfare of both marriage partners is considered in the family's decision to migrate. However, the effect of wife's unemployment on migration is statistically significant only between 1971 and 1973. Nationally, unemployment rates were higher during this period than in the 1968 to 1970 period.

The statistically significant retarding effect of both the wife's and the husband's receipt of unemployment compensation in the 1968 to 1970 and 1971 to 1973 equations of table 6-1 is subject to two interpretations.[16] In the first place, since persons who voluntarily quit their previous jobs are usually ineligible for unemployment compensation, it seems that persons who lose their jobs because of a layoff or discharge are less likely to move than persons who become unemployed as a result of their own volition. Second, it may indicate that persons who receive unemployment compensation are not familiar with the interstate migration provisions of the unemployment compensation system—that is, some persons who receive compensation will not want to risk losing their payments because of an interstate move.[17]

Tables 6-2 and 6-3 simply transform the equations of table 6-1 into more readable form. All the preceding results are illustrated. For instance, column 1 of table 6-2 suggests that the likelihood of migration is negatively related to the length of the wife's tenure at her current job.

The likelihood of migration between 1968 and 1970 and between 1971 and 1973 was 16.5 percent and 17 percent, respectively. Apparently, the migration-inducing effect of a cyclical downturn (the greater migration propensity of the unemployed as compared with the employed) is offset by the migration-retarding effect of the reduction in voluntary quits. This result may well be due to the mildness of the cyclical downturn.

However, the underlying determinants of migration listed in table 6-1 appear to change over the business cycle. The variable reflecting "taste for migration" (wife attended a nonlocal college) is a significant positive determinant of migration during all phases of the business cycle.[18] Yet, several variables

**Table 6-2**

**Percentage of White Respondents' Families who Migrated Between 1968 and 1973 by Respondent's Employment Status, Job Tenure, and College Location[a]**

| Employment Status and Job Tenure | Did Not Attend College | Attended College | |
|---|---|---|---|
| | | Local College | Nonlocal College |
| Out of labor force | 26.7 | 30.3 | 40.8 |
| Employed | | | |
| 1 year | 21.4 | 24.5 | 34.0 |
| 2 years | 16.9 | 19.5 | 27.8 |

[a]Calculated on the basis of the original logit coefficients for a family with the sample means for all characteristics other than wife's 1968 survey week job tenure and college location. Information on the original logit model is available from the authors.

influencing the monetary gains from migration (respondent's unemployment, husband's education, and husband's receipt of unemployment compensation) are significant only during the business downturn. Also, the signs of the variables reflecting husband's age and local-area unemployment rate are consistent with economic theory only during the cyclical downturn. Apparently, variables influencing the financial remuneration of migration are more important during times of economic stagnation than during periods of prosperity.[19] Indeed, 47 percent of the migrants during the 1971 to 1973 period reported moving for "economic" reasons (unemployment, steadier work, better job, and so on) as compared with only 38 percent in the 1968 to 1970 period.

The 1968 to 1973 regressions in table 6-1 were also run for a sample of 118 blacks. The coefficients of wife's tenure and employment status, and husband's education, all hypothesized to be correlated with the expected income return from migration, were nonsignificant. Apparently, blacks respond less than whites to the expected income gain from migration. Bowles' findings were similar.[20] He offered as an explanation evidence that blacks are more risk averse and discount the future more than whites.

*The Effect of Migration on Earnings*

The coefficient of the dummy variable representing migration status, in a regression where the dependent variable is change in labor market earnings, represents the change in earnings associated with migration. By controlling for personal characteristics (that is, age and education) and base year earnings, we isolate the net effect of migration on earnings.[21] Table 6-4 summarizes the regression results when the dependent variables are change in the husband's, respondent's, family's, and single woman's earnings and respondent's weeks worked.

Table 6-3

**Percentage of White Respondents' Families who Migrated Between 1968 and 1970 and 1971 and 1973 by Employment Status of Respondent and Husband[a]**

| Respondent's Employment Status | Migration 1968-1970 | | | | Migration 1971-1973 | | | |
|---|---|---|---|---|---|---|---|---|
| | Number of Weeks Worked by Husband, 1967 | | | Husband Received Unemployment Compensation | Number of Weeks Worked by Husband, 1970 | | | Husband Received Unemployment Compensation |
| | 52 | 40 | 30 | | 52 | 40 | 30 | |
| Unemployed | | | | | | | | |
| Without compensation | 22.5 | 26.7 | 31.0 | 19.6 | 30.4 | 36.4 | 43.3 | 22.2 |
| With compensation | 6.4 | 7.9 | 9.5 | 5.4 | 11.8 | 14.9 | 18.9 | 8.0 |
| All others | 14.7 | 17.7 | 21.0 | 12.6 | 13.8 | 17.4 | 21.9 | 9.5 |

[a]Calculated on the basis of the original logit coefficients in the 1968-1970 (1971-1973) migration equations, for a family with the sample means for all characteristics other than wife's and husband's receipt of unemployment compensation over the past year and husband's 1967 (1970) weeks worked. Information on the original logit models is available from the authors.

## Table 6-4
### Growth of Migrant, Relative to Nonmigrant, Annual Earnings (in 1968 Dollars) and in Weeks Worked per Year Between 1969 and 1973 by Marital Status: Regression Results[a]

| Migrant Characteristics[b] | Married Women[c] | | | Change in Family Earnings | | Single Women[d] Change in Earnings |
|---|---|---|---|---|---|---|
| | Change in Husband's Earnings | Change in Respondent's Earnings | Change in Respondent's Weeks Worked | Husband's Variables | Respondent's Variables | |
| Year of migration | | | | | | |
| Between 1969 and 1972 survey dates | 324 | −515** | −6.6*** | −106 | 66 | 1218** |
| Between 1969 and 1971 survey dates | 770* | −405 | −5.0* | 413 | 629 | |
| Reason for migration | | | | | | |
| Economic | 1064** | −367 | −4.1 | 971* | 1409* | |
| Noneconomic | −355 | −552** | −6.4** | −1008** | −1049** | |

a1969 (1973) earnings are defined as earnings over the twelve-month period preceding the 1969 (1973) survey date.

bIf the dependent variable is change in husband's earnings, the control variables are husband's age, education, and 1969 earnings. If change in wife's or single female's earnings is the dependent variable, the control variables correspond to her age, education, and 1969 earnings.

cUniverse consists of 357 white married respondents. For all survey years (1968 to 1973), the following restrictions apply: same spouse is present, and neither respondent nor husband is enrolled in school. Thus there may be a few husbands over age twenty-five enrolled in school in the sample. Respondents included in the sample must have lived at their 1969 SMSA or county of residence at least two years, and their husbands must have worked full time in 1969 and 1973.

dUniverse consists of 107 white respondents, never married and not enrolled in school in all survey years. Respondents must have lived in 1969 SMSA or county of residence at least two years to be included in sample.

*Significant at the 10 percent level.

**Significant at the 5 percent level.

***Significant at the 1 percent level.

The control variables in the regression equations summarized in table 6-4 are worthy of some discussion. A negative effect for age and a positive effect for years of schooling are predicted by the theory of human capital. Since the dependent variable is the change in earnings, we are actually examining the experience/earnings profile. Theory suggests that investment in on-the-job training is positively associated with education and negatively associated with age. Therefore, it is expected that younger and more educated individuals will exhibit, ceteris paribus, faster earnings growth than their older and/or less educated counterparts. Since in theory the propensity to migrate is positively associated with education and negatively associated with age, omission of education and age from the change in earnings equation would theoretically lead to an overstatement of the returns to migration.[22]

First, consider the impact of migration between 1969 and 1972 on 1973 earnings. The regression results suggest that the effect of migration on the husband's earnings is positive, although the migration coefficient is never statistically significant. Migration has a negative and statistically significant effect on the wife's earnings. Migration does not improve family (husband plus wife) earnings.

For a single woman, migration will theoretically occur only if the move is expected to increase her utility. Since this condition does not necessarily hold for married women or any individual member of multiperson households, we would expect to observe, on the average, a greater increase in personal welfare due to migration for single than for married women. While own earnings may not be a good proxy for the welfare of a married woman, change in earnings may be regarded as a first approximation to change in welfare for a single woman who usually works full time. Our results are considered with this line of reasoning. Ceteris paribus, between 1969 and 1973, single female migrants registered earnings gains of $1,200 more than single nonmigrants.

To provide some insight into the source of the earnings loss for migrant married women, we regressed the change in annual weeks worked between the 1969 and 1973 surveys on migration dummy variables and the number of weeks worked in the twelve months prior to the 1969 survey date (table 6-4). The statistically significant negative coefficient for the 1969 to 1972 migration dummy indicates that the slower growth in the earnings of migrant wives, as compared with nonmobile women, is due to reduced market work. Multiplying the respondent's average 1968 weekly earnings ($148) by the decline in annual weeks worked following migration (6.6), we can more than explain the decline in their earnings shown in table 6-4.

Comparison of the coefficient for migration between 1969 and 1972 with that for migration between 1969 and 1971 suggests that the difference in weeks worked between migrant and nonmigrant married women narrows with the passing of time. This implies that the initial reduced work effort represents a cost of migration for the wife rather than a change in taste for work by migrants.

It seems that, from the family viewpoint, the migrant wife often foregoes immediate market work to set up the new household and search for a desirable job. In fact, after two years in their new residences, the earnings of migrant wives are not significantly different from those of nonmigrant wives.

The observed effect of migration on individual and family earnings does not appear to support our model. Perhaps the small earnings increase for husbands and the lack of change in family earnings between 1969 and 1973 from migration are short-run phenomena. Important postmigration on-the-job training (at the cost of temporarily lower earnings) could be occurring at this stage of the life cycle, in which case migration might be beneficial in the long run. Indeed, the effect of 1969 to 1971 migration on the husband's 1973 earnings was positive and significant at the 10 percent level. Moreover, the effect of 1969 to 1971 migration on the family's 1973 earnings was positive, but nonsignificant.

It must be remembered that our model has ignored noneconomic aspects of migration and some families undoubtedly migrated for nonpecuniary reasons. In this connection note that husband's and family's earnings registered substantial gains (around $1,000) in those cases where respondents claimed to have migrated for "economic reasons." Conversely, those who migrated for "noneconomic reasons" were willing to sacrifice, on the average, $1,000, or 12 percent of total family earnings in exchange for the presumed nonpecuniary benefits of their new residence (table 6-4).[23]

### Summary and Conclusions

In this chapter several determinants of family migration have been examined. First, it is clear that the labor market orientation of married women enters family decisions to migrate. Second, families in which either the husband or wife experiences unemployment are more likely to be geographically mobile than other families. Third, migration seems to be more closely associated with economic variables (for example, age, education, unemployment, and labor supply) when overall economic conditions are poor. Finally, attendees of nonlocal colleges are more likely to ultimately settle in communities other than their "hometown" than persons who attend local colleges.

The observed effect of migration on individual and family earnings often does not support our model. Perhaps the small earnings increase for husbands and the inconsequential effect of migration on family earnings between 1969 and 1973 are short-run phenomena. Important on-the-job training often takes place at this stage of the life cycle that may make migration beneficial in the long run even when no short-run benefits are evident. The earnings loss to migrant wives diminishes over time as their labor supply increases.

We observe significant differences in the effect of migration on the earnings of single compared with married women. This chapter, we believe, is the first documentation of the earnings gain to unmarried women who migrate. They gain $1,200 per year more than nonmigrants, while migrant wives earn $500 per year less than their nonmobile counterparts.

## Notes

1. The current framework resembles one presented by the authors in a previous study of the migration of mature women [Steven H. Sandell, "The Economics of Family Migration," in *Dual Careers*, vol. IV (Columbus: The Ohio State University, Center for Human Resource Research, December 1975)].

2. While the authors acknowledge the many noneconomic aspects of migration, this chapter is primarily concerned with the economic aspects.

3. We make the simplifying assumption that family income only consists of the labor market earnings of the husband and wife. Inclusion of nonlabor income or labor market earnings of other family members would not change the conclusions. Also, the demand for hours of leisure is assumed to be related to the inverse of the supply of hours of work which is priced at the wage rate and, therefore, is not nonpecuniary as might be first thought.

4. Julie DaVanzo, *Why Families Move* (Washington, D.C.: U.S. Government Printing Office, 1977).

5. An unemployed migrant can continue to collect unemployment insurance benefits from his original area of residence. See U.S. Department of Labor, Manpower Administration, Unemployment Insurance Service, *Comparison of State Unemployment Insurance Laws* (Washington, D.C.: U.S. Government Printing Office, 1973).

6. Donald O. Parsons, "Quit Rates Over Time: A Search and Information Approach," *American Economic Review* (June 1973):390-401.

7. This assumes that some of the employed believe employment prospects are better elsewhere. The literature on the effect of the business cycle on migration is sparse. Hope T. Eldridge, "A Cohort Approach to the Analysis of Migration Differentials," *Demography* 1 (1964):212-219, found that U.S. migration fell precipitously during the Great Depression years. Joseph Shister, "Labor Mobility: Some Institutional Aspects," *Industrial Relations Research Association Proceedings of Third Annual Meeting* (1950):42-59, noted the variations in labor mobility related to the business cycles of the 1930s and 1940s. International migration is also influenced by the business cycle [Harry Jerome, *Migration and Business Cycles* (New York: National Bureau of Economic Research, 1926)].

8. Assuming a given migration is final, the difference in current incomes before and after migration is a valid proxy for the present value of returns to migration, since the two are highly correlated (Aba Schwartz, "Migration and Life Span Earnings in the U.S.," Ph.D. dissertation, University of Chicago, 1968).

9. Because of the econometric problems associated with estimation when the dependent variable can only take the values of 0 or 1 [Henri Theil, *Principles of Econometrics* (New York: John Wiley and Sons, 1971), pp. 632-633], logit analysis is used. The dependent variable is converted to the natural log of the relative probability of migration (that is, $ln \frac{p}{1-p}$).

10. Approximately 34 percent (269) of the families of white married women (same spouse present all survey years) are migrants under this definition. Between 1968 and 1973, 61 percent of the migrants moved more than 100 miles and 65 percent moved more than 50 miles. We should caution the reader that in all four NLS cohorts, errors in some of the variables representing comparisons of areas of residence have been found. These errors are being corrected by a Census Bureau check on the addresses recorded on the interview schedules.

11. Samuel Bowles, "Migration as Investment: Empirical Tests of the Human Investment Approach to Geographic Mobility," *The Review of Economics and Statistics* 52 (November 1970):356-362, and Schwartz, "Migration and Life Span Earnings" explain the positive correlation between migration rates and educational level by hypothesizing that individuals with more education have better access to labor market information for distant regions. Furthermore, according to human capital theory, persons with more human capital are more productive in seeking investment alternatives. So, considering migration as an investment, the more educated should be more responsive to interarea wage differentials.

12. U.S. Department of Labor, Employment and Training Administration, *Employment and Training Report of the President* (Washington, D.C.: U.S. Government Printing Office, 1976), p. 389. Since the NLS interviews with the young women were conducted between January and April of each year, the 1968 to 1970 time span covers early 1968 to early 1970. The 1971 to 1973 time span covers early 1971 to early 1973.

13. Husband's age was nonsignificant and often exhibited the theoretically wrong sign. It was hypothesized that the coefficient for husband's age would be negative, since the length of time for a person to reap benefits from moving decreases with age. However, Gary S. Becker's illustrative calculations in *Human Capital: A Theoretical and Empirical Analysis, with Special Reference to Education*, National Bureau of Economic Research (New York: Columbia University Press, 1964) indicate that returns received twenty years after an investment are so heavily discounted that they do not substantially influence the rate of return on the investment. Thus, for our very young sample where the average age of the husbands is twenty-five, it is not surprising that the differences in propensities to migrate for different ages of the husband should be unsubstantial.

14. The coefficients of the respondent's labor force commitment variables were nonsignificant and positive for the separate 1968 to 1970 and 1971 to

1973 migration equations. The apparent difference between the results for the two-year time span equations and the results for the 1968 to 1973 equations may be due to the husbands, on the average, being older over the 1968 to 1973 regression sample period than over the two-year regression sample periods—that is, in the 1968 to 1970, 1971 to 1973, and 1968 to 1973 equations, the respondent is between the ages of seventeen and twenty-four *at the beginning* of each of the respective periods. Thus the average age of the husbands at the end of the period examined in the 1968 to 1973 regressions is thirty-three, while it is only twenty-nine at the end of the periods spanning 1968 to 1970 and 1971 to 1973. Using Census data, Jacob Mincer, "Family Migration Decision," mimeographed, January 1976, and Larry H. Long, "Women's Labor Force Participation and the Residential Mobility of Families," *Social Forces* 52 (March 1974):342-349, found that the *simple* correlation between the wife's labor force commitment and migration was negative only when the husband was over age thirty. Long hypothesized that only after the husband had become established in his career did the wife's employment reduce his willingness to migrate.

Variables reflecting work expectations ("does respondent plan to be working at age thirty-five?") and fertility plans of working wives in 1968 were also examined. They were not significant determinants of migration.

15. The coefficients of the wife's nonlocal college dummy variables were statistically different from the coefficients of the local college dummy variables at the 10 percent level. For the 1968 to 1970 equation, the coefficients were statistically different at the 1 percent level.

Further analysis showed that a substantially higher percentage of nonlocal as compared with local college attendees do not live in their high-school area of residence after college. In 1968 68 percent of the married respondents who attended a nonlocal college did not live in their high-school area of residence. The corresponding figure for those attending local colleges was 29 percent. Of course, rural high-school students are more likely to attend nonlocal colleges and to leave their high-school area of residence after college. This phenomenon could explain the positive association between nonlocal college attendance and a postcollege residence different from one's high-school residence. However, the positive association remained when the sample was restricted to those respondents who at age fourteen resided in a city of over 25,000.

16. The coefficients were statistically significant only at the 10 percent level. Preferable to a variable measuring receipt of unemployment compensation sometime during the *year previous* to the migration period would have been a measure of the husband's and the wife's receipt of unemployment compensation *immediately prior* to the relevant migration period. Thus the coefficients of the unemployment compensation variables are biased toward zero, which could account for the low level of significance.

17. The "push" effect of the local unemployment rate on out-migration was never significant. Using *aggregate* interarea migration data, John B. Lansing

and Eva Mueller, *The Geographic Mobility of Labor*, (Ann Arbor, Mich.: Institute for Social Research, 1967); W.J. Wadycki, "Alternative Opportunities and Interstate Migration: Some Additional Results," *Review of Economics and Statistics* 56 (May 1974):254-257; and Ira S. Lowry, *Migration and Metropolitan Growth: Two Analytical Models* (San Francisco: Chandler Publishing Company, 1966), among others, reported similar findings. Many of these studies used the end-of-period local unemployment rate to analyze migration over the period. But migration will influence the end-of-period unemployment rate. This simultaneous equation bias could have accounted for the failure of unemployment to influence migration in the single equation models of past studies. We avoid this difficulty by using microdata to examine the effect of beginning-of-period unemployment on migration over the period.

18. The difference between the coefficients for the dummy variables representing local and nonlocal college attendance represents the effect of nonlocal college attendance on migration.

19. The only variable with a coefficient that is significantly different (at the 5 percent level) between the two time periods is husband's education.

At the 1 percent level a Chow test rejected the null hypothesis that the underlying determinants of migration between 1968 and 1970 were the same as the determinants between 1971 and 1973. The Chow test was performed on the ordinary least squares (OLS) equivalents to the 1968 to 1970 and 1971 to 1973 equations in table 6-1. The OLS and logit equations were very similar.

20. See Bowles, "Migration as Investment."

21. Lack of data on a migrant's job situation immediately prior to migration (that is, whether he or she had been or was likely to be fired or laid off) forced us to assume that the premigration earnings stream would have persisted in the absence of migration. If this premigration earnings stream would not have persisted (for example, the migrant had been fired or laid off), then we understate returns to migration.

22. The signs of some of the coefficients of the control variables—age and education—are ostensibly inconsistent with expectation. However, the only one of these coefficients that is statistically significant is the negative coefficient of wife's education in the equation with change in the wife's earnings as the dependent variable. On further reflection even this is not necessarily inconsistent with human capital theory. Belton M. Fleisher in "Mother's Home Time and the Production of Child Quality," *Demography* 14 (May 1977):197-212, found that schooling increases a mother's productivity in producing child "quality" (defined by IQ, schooling, and postschool wage of the child) more than it increases her market productivity. This would explain Arleen S. Leibowitz's finding in "Women's Allocation of Time to Market and Nonmarket Activities: Differences by Education," Ph.D. dissertation, Columbia University, 1972, that better educated women are more likely than their less-educated counterparts to reduce their labor force participation when they have children. This, in turn, could

explain our negative education coefficient in the wife's change in earnings equation.

23. However, it must be acknowledged that since migrants were asked why they migrated *after* the migration, their responses may be rationalizations of economic disappointments.

# 7

# The Causes and Consequences of Marital Breakdown

*Frank L. Mott* and
*Sylvia F. Moore*

In this volume we have already highlighted a number of phenomena that reflect in major ways the changing status of women in American society. We have repeatedly demonstrated the increasing work commitment of women. It is clear that for young adult women work is and will continue to be a complementary and essential component of contemporary family life styles and not an alternative to family and child raising.

Paralleling many fundamental changes in our society, the increasing work activity of women in some instances has been both a determinant and consequence of other social phenomena. The process of marital disruption is a case in point. The ability to find remunerative employment can certainly facilitate and possibly increase the likelihood of a marital breakdown for some women. Thus work or the potential for finding work may play the dual role of affecting the probability of marital breakdown and of ameliorating the economic trauma associated with the breakdown after it occurs.

The major objective of this chapter is to examine the association between work and the process of marital breakdown. Since this association cannot be analyzed in a vacuum, a wide range of other factors are considered when we examine the determinants of the marital disruption process. When the consequences of a marital breakdown are analyzed, labor market activity will be juxtaposed against the needs of different subsets of women. Obviously, work is only one way of compensating for the loss of the husband's earnings and needs to be considered in conjunction with access to other income sources.

Recent years have witnessed a spiralling of the incidence of marital breakdown from what had been rather low and stable levels historically. During the period between 1900 and 1965, the divorce rate rose from 0.7 to 2.5 per 1,000 population.[1] However, during the following ten-year period the rate virtually doubled from 2.5 to 4.9 per thousand population.[2]

Perhaps the most dramatic changes in marital disruption patterns are occurring today. There has been a dramatic increase in the proportion of marriages estimated to end in divorce among successive generations of contemporary women. The Census Bureau estimates that about one-third of the marriages of young women now between the ages of twenty-five and thirty-four will ultimately end in divorce, as compared with about 20 percent of those who

The authors wish to thank Dennis Grey for his outstanding research assistance in producing this chapter.

are currently in their fifties.[3] Indeed, during the short five-year period between 1968 and 1973, fully 14 percent of the married young women (12 percent of the white and 30 percent of the black women) in our nationally representative National Longitudinal Surveys' (NLS) sample had their marriages end either permanently through a divorce or at least temporarily through a separation. To the extent that these new higher levels of marital breakdown may partially represent a break with traditional disruption patterns, this study may provide useful baseline data for interpreting several socioeconomic dimensions of contemporary marital trends.

It is evident that marital disruption is no longer a relatively rare phenomenon. In reality, it either affects or will affect a considerable proportion of women who are currently young adults. As such, there is a need for a clear definition of public policies with respect to income maintenance and employment assistance for this substantial group of women. However, the effective determination and implementation of any social policy requires information input, including analytical evidence concerning the sociodemographic makeup of the program group as well as quantitative indications of its economic status. A principal objective of this chapter is to provide some of this essential input.

## Some Data and Analytical Constraints

Our sample of maritally disrupted women includes all women who will either separate or divorce for the first time between 1968 and 1973.[4] Since the precise date of separation cannot be determined for most women, the "before" and "after" status will refer to the nearest interview date before and after the marital disruption. Throughout this study $T$ will reference the last interview before the disruption; $T + 1$, the first interview after the event; and $T - 1$ and $T + 2$, the immediately earlier and later interview dates.

To compare the characteristics of individuals in our sample whose marriages were disrupted with a comparable group whose marriages remained intact, a "reference group" representing "nondisrupting counterparts" (to those whose marriages broke down) was constructed. In the most general terms, a woman was included in the reference group if she was in her first marriage at some point between 1968 and 1973 and the marriage did not break up during that period.[5]

To maximize our sample size we are examining the determinants and consequences of marital disruption rather than the separate divorce or separation components. We feel that this is justified in most instances since the *short-term* social and economic consequences of both events are similar. In both cases the husband is absent from and no longer a member of the household. In the short run the determinants of marital breakdown should also be similar, regardless of whether the process results in a quick divorce or a more lingering separation process.

Given the nature of our sample, the perspective of this paper is from the female side—that is, we focus on why a woman separates from or is divorced from her husband and what the postdisruption consequences are for her and those living with her. Clearly, the husband's perspective might be quite different, both in terms of the determinants and consequences of the marital disruption. While to some extent certain mirror images are implied, symmetry in all instances is not suggested.

Finally, the nature of the data limits and perhaps biases the focus of our research, particularly with regard to the interpretation of the determinants and consequences of the marital disruption. We are essentially measuring in a discrete way a process that is, in reality, continuous. For example, the factors that we find to be significant "determinants" of marital disruption may well reflect precipitating events in the disruption process rather than true causes of disruption. As such, we are recording overt manifestations of a much more subtle process.

## The Marital Disruption Process

As a mechanism for better understanding the socioeconomic position of women from broken marriages, this section examines some of the suggested motives for marital disruption. Subject to the constraints and limitations of our data set, we test some of the traditional, as well as more recent theoretical statements found in both the economic and sociological literature concerning the likelihood of marital disruption among women. As our sample represents a cross section of young adult women, our results may be more broadly applicable and more readily generalized than those of other studies based on more limited samples.

The literature that focuses on the determinants of marital disruption has expanded greatly in recent years and has become increasingly interdisciplinary in nature. From the sociological perspective, the effects of background factors such as the socioeconomic status, education, and marital stability of parents in the promotion of marital stability of their children have been explored in some depth.[6] Generally, studies have found inverse associations between the probability of marital disruption and background socioeconomic status variables and educational attainment. There is also some suggestion of a transmission of intergenerational marital stability, as some studies indicate that children of broken marriages are more likely to have their own marriages dissolve.

Demographers have noted that marriages undertaken at youthful ages, particularly those burdened by premaritally conceived children, usually tend to have less chance of success.[7] On the other hand, economists or those working primarily with economic variables have most recently been focusing on the various economic motivations for marital breakdown. These include such factors as the absolute level of the family's income prior to the marital disruption, the relative position of the family compared with peers, and the level of the woman's earnings preceding the disruption event.[8]

It is apparent that many of the factors that traditionally have been considered by researchers from different disciplines in reality overlap in the sense of being interdependent in origin and interactive in their effects on marital breakdown and its consequences. Indeed, a principal objective of the multivariate perspective of this research is to suggest which of a myriad of background factors may be the truly significant determinants of the disruption process.

Because the major purpose of this study is to examine the relevance of work activity and concomitant economic factors in the disruption process, we concentrate more extensively on the background factors explored in the economics literature. We attempt to distinguish those economic factors that are felt to contribute to marital disintegration from those economic factors hypothesized to "cement" a marriage. Ross and Sawhill term these forces "independence" and "income" effects.[9] From an economic perspective, factors that would promote a feeling of economic independence in a woman, such as high-wage employment or access to unearned income independent of her husband, might, everything else being equal, provide encouragement for a woman to leave a marriage. In contrast, factors that encourage a wife's dependence on her husband, such as his high earnings or substantial personal unearned income, are "income effects" that would normally be associated with below average probabilities of marital breakdown.

In addition to these absolute income and earnings concepts, relative concepts also appear in the economics literature, such as the relationship of the wife's actual or expected earnings[10] to changes in the husband's earnings over time,[11] and the ratio of the husband's actual to his expected earnings.[12] Relatively high husband's earnings in comparison with (1) past periods, (2) his "expected" earnings, and (3) his wife's earnings would be expected to be associated with a below average likelihood of marital disruption.

An examination of table 7-1 suggests that there are indeed major socioeconomic differences between maritally disrupted and nondisrupted ("reference") families. Women in stable (nondisrupted) families had higher family income, were less likely to be receiving public assistance, and were better educated. From a relative perspective, their families were more likely to have improved their financial situation during the preceding year (between $T - 1$ and $T$). Aside from the direct economic factors, women from stable backgrounds (living with both parents at age fourteen) as well as women living in smaller families (with fewer children of their own) had lower marital disruption probabilities. Similar patterns are evidenced for both black and white women. However, blacks, regardless of whether their marriages were disrupted or remained stable, had lower levels of economic well-being than whites.

*Some Multivariate Results*

To estimate the independent influence of the various socioeconomic and demographic factors on the probability of marital disruption, a multivariate model incorporating a variety of relevant variables was constructed. The multivariate technique employed is multiple classification analysis (MCA), a form of regression analysis using dummy variables. With MCA we can determine for relevant categories of a certain independent variable that proportion of young women which subsequently experienced marital disruption, assuming that members of that category have an "average value" on all other variables included in the analysis. Differences in the proportions disrupted among the variable's categories are interpreted as the "pure" association of that variable with the probability of undergoing marital disruption.

The dependent variable is dichotomous, with a value of 1 given to those respondents whose marriages were first disrupted between 1968 and 1973, and a 0 if the respondent was at some point during this period eligible to have a marital disruption but did not do so (our previously defined "reference" group).

The full multivariate model that estimates the probability of marital disruption for black and white women includes a range of socioeconomic and demographic variables that are felt to be significant predictors of marital disruption (see table 7-2). The proxies for the "independence effect" are the woman's potential wage (a constructed variable that estimates a woman's potential hourly earnings based on a number of her personal characteristics[13]); her access to welfare (primarily Aid to Families with Dependent Children) payments; her labor market experience as measured by the number of years in which she has worked six months or more since leaving school; and the number of hours she worked during the survey week at time $T$.

While none of these variables attains significance as a predictor of marital breakdown for both races, there are several variables that seem to affect one race but not the other. Hours worked in the survey week and years of work experience are significant predictors of marital disruption for white women, but are not for blacks. Of the two, only the work experience variable approaches significance for the black respondents. Conversely, only accessibility to welfare attains a high level of significance for the black women and, although it is not significant for whites, it does operate in the right direction. In general, empirical evidence consistent with the hypothesized "independence effect" is moderately significant for whites but marginal at best for black respondents.

The primary "income effect" variable in our model is husband's earnings. Presumably, higher earnings by the husband, everything else being equal, should be associated with lower levels of marital disruption. In addition, lower family debt levels would also be expected to be associated with more stable marriages.

**Table 7-1**
**Characteristics of Marital Disruption and Reference Groups at Time** $T$**, by Race**

| Characteristics | Reference Group | | Marital Disruptees | |
|---|---|---|---|---|
| | Whites | Blacks | Whites | Blacks |
| Work related | | | | |
| Labor force participation rate | 56.0 | 58.5 | 54.9 | 56.4 |
| Unemployment rate | 10.8 | 17.9 | 12.5 | 29.4 |
| Median Duncan Index of current or last job | 44.2 | 22.4 | 37.9 | 19.1 |
| Percent (of employed) employed full time | 69.3 | 75.0 | 75.5 | 88.7 |
| Husband's weeks worked in past year (percent with less than 26 weeks) | 9.5 | 4.8 | 8.5 | 9.1 |
| Mean hourly wage of current or last job | 2.03 | 1.71 | 1.79 | 1.64 |
| Income asset | | | | |
| Median family income | 7,797 | 6,296 | 7,095 | 5,700 |
| Median respondent's earnings | 1,169 | 844 | 833 | 982 |
| Mean family income | 8,232 | 6,890 | 7,522 | 6,251 |
| Mean respondent's earnings | 1,982 | 1,608 | 1,708 | 1,594 |
| Percent with liabilities (excluding 30-day charge) | 43.0 | 49.3 | 59.0 | 46.9 |
| Percent owning own home | 26.9 | 17.6 | 32.6 | 19.7 |
| Percent with improving finances between $T-1$ and $T$ | 57.8 | 54.3 | 48.8 | 32.4 |
| Percent with family member receiving public assistance | 2.5 | 7.7 | 5.4 | 17.3 |
| Family related | | | | |
| Mean family size | 2.97 | 4.14 | 3.25 | 4.54 |
| Percent with own children | 48.6 | 68.3 | 61.4 | 83.4 |
| Duration of marriage (percent married less than 3.5 years) | 69.5 | 73.7 | 53.1 | 55.1 |
| Personal | | | | |
| Percent with less than 12 years of school | 17.8 | 35.3 | 38.8 | 56.4 |
| Percent who lived with both parents at age 14 | 85.1 | 61.4 | 75.6 | 51.3 |
| Median age | 22.3 | 22.1 | 21.7 | 21.8 |

Finally, in a relative context, one would expect greater marital stability in those marriages where the family financial status has been stable or improving.

There was no substantial association between husband's earnings and marital stability for either blacks or whites. For whites, however, having no accumulated debts was associated with lower levels of marital disruption. Finally, recent

**Table 7-2**

**Unadjusted and Adjusted Proportions of Respondents Experiencing a Marital Disruption Between 1968 and 1973, by Race: Multiple Classification Analysis[a]**

| Characteristics | Whites | | | Blacks | | |
|---|---|---|---|---|---|---|
| | Number of Respondents | Unadjusted Proportion | Adjusted Proportion | Number of Respondents | Unadjusted Proportion | Adjusted Proportion |
| Age of youngest child | | | | | | |
| 0-1 years | 650 | .14 | .12 | 289 | .35 | .33 |
| 2 or more years | 382 | .16 | .14 | 135 | .36 | .32 |
| No children | 998 | .10 | .12 | 168 | .20 | .28 |
| Accessibility of welfare in state[b] | | | *** | | | ** |
| Low access - low benefits | 551 | .14 | .11 | 331 | .28 | .27 |
| High access - high benefits | 812 | .12 | .14 | 165 | .34 | .35 |
| Other | 667 | .12 | .12 | 96 | .37 | .40 |
| Respondent's education | | | *** | | | ** |
| 0-11 years | 444 | .24 | .20 | 254 | .41 | .38 |
| 12 years | 1,093 | .11 | .11 | 264 | .26 | .26 |
| 13 or more years | 493 | .06 | .10 | 74 | .19 | .28 |
| Debt accumulation | | | * | | | |
| No debt | 577 | .09 | .11 | 167 | .28 | .31 |
| Some debt | 604 | .15 | .15 | 198 | .30 | .30 |
| Not ascertainable | 849 | .13 | .12 | 227 | .35 | .33 |
| Work experience | | | *** | | | |
| 0-2 years | 1,202 | .12 | .11 | 394 | .32 | .29 |
| 3 or more years | 828 | .13 | .15 | 198 | .30 | .35 |
| Potential wage[b] | | | | | | |
| $1.50 or less | 658 | .18 | .16 | 271 | .32 | .29 |
| $1.51-1.99 | 643 | .11 | .11 | 207 | .36 | .35 |
| $2.00 or more | 729 | .10 | .11 | 114 | .22 | .30 |
| Residence in SMSA | | | *** | | | |
| Yes | 1,239 | .13 | .14 | 391 | .31 | .32 |
| No | 791 | .11 | .10 | 201 | .32 | .29 |

**Table 7-2** (cont.)

| Characteristics | Whites | | | Blacks | | |
|---|---|---|---|---|---|---|
| | Number of Respondents | Unadjusted Proportion | Adjusted Proportion | Number of Respondents | Unadjusted Proportion | Adjusted Proportion |
| Husband's earnings in past year | | | * | | | ** |
| $0-3,999 | 640 | .12 | .12 | 248 | .31 | .30 |
| $4,000-5,999 | 448 | .14 | .13 | 155 | .30 | .31 |
| $6,000-7,999 | 411 | .11 | .11 | 75 | .23 | .24 |
| $8,000 or more | 370 | .11 | .11 | 35 | .22 | .28 |
| Not ascertainable | 161 | .17 | .19 | 79 | .49 | .45 |
| Both parents present at age 14 | | | ** | | | |
| Yes | 1,698 | .11 | .12 | 342 | .27 | .29 |
| No | 332 | .19 | .16 | 250 | .37 | .34 |
| Age of respondent | | | *** | | | ** |
| 15-19 | 316 | .18 | .19 | 124 | .37 | .42 |
| 20-21 | 483 | .13 | .14 | 143 | .30 | .31 |
| 22-23 | 576 | .11 | .12 | 158 | .27 | .28 |
| 24 or older | 655 | .10 | .09 | 167 | .32 | .27 |
| Duration of marriage | | | *** | | | *** |
| 0-1½ years | 948 | .09 | .08 | 305 | .21 | .22 |
| 2-2½ years | 238 | .17 | .16 | 73 | .38 | .35 |
| 3-5 years | 525 | .17 | .18 | 136 | .47 | .47 |
| 5½ or more years | 319 | .13 | .15 | 78 | .31 | .34 |
| Ease of divorce: divorce rate in state[b] | | | *** | | | |
| 0-2.6 | 484 | .09 | .10 | 84 | .37 | .32 |
| 2.7-4.1 | 535 | .10 | .10 | 228 | .33 | .36 |
| 4.2-6.7 | 579 | .15 | .14 | 177 | .28 | .28 |
| 6.8 or higher | 181 | .20 | .20 | 65 | .29 | .27 |
| Not ascertainable | 251 | .12 | .15 | 38 | .29 | .30 |

| | | | *** | | | *** |
|---|---|---|---|---|---|---|
| Change in financial position $T-1$ to $T$ | | | | | | |
| Better | 992 | .11 | .11 | 241 | .20 | .24 |
| Same | 606 | .15 | .14 | 220 | .36 | .33 |
| Worse | 182 | .14 | .14 | 61 | .39 | .35 |
| Not ascertainable | 250 | .14 | .13 | 70 | .47 | .48 |
| Hours worked during survey week | | | *** | | | |
| None reported | 1,076 | .13 | .10 | 347 | .36 | .33 |
| 1-34 | 283 | .11 | .13 | 59 | .18 | .22 |
| 35 or more | 671 | .13 | .16 | 186 | .27 | .31 |
| Grand mean | 2,030 | .13 | .13 | 592 | .31 | .31 |
| $R^2$ | | | .06*** | | | .12*** |

aRespondents fourteen to twenty-four years of age in 1968 who have either experienced a first marital disruption or who are included in the reference group.

bFor a complete description of this variable, see appendix 7A.

*Significant at the 10 percent level.

**Significant at the 5 percent level.

***Significant at the 1 percent level.

improvements in financial position (between $T - 1$ and $T$) were associated with lower probabilities of marital disruption for both races. However, the association was significant only for blacks. This suggests that to the extent that economic factors are relevant, concepts that measure changes in a family's economic status relative to long-term norms appear to be of greater importance than status variables referencing one point in time.

In contrast to the only moderate significance of the economic variables, demographic and social variables associated with the woman's background are important predictors of marital breakdown. For both black and white women, the negative association between education and marital disruption probabilities is highly significant. That this inverse relationship persists even after controlling for the economic correlates of educational attainment indicates that higher levels of schooling bear an independent relationship to a propensity for marital stability.

Consistent with the literature, being raised in a broken home is found to be positively associated with marital disruption even with all the other socio-economic controls in the model. Thus there may be certain social-psychological syndromes among blacks and whites that tend to pass on a "propensity to disrupt" from one generation to the next.

Also note that for both black and white women there remains a strong inverse association between age and marital disruption, even after controlling for all the other factors that are known to be associated with aging per se. Indeed, the data suggest that any institutional means that can be used to raise significantly the age of marriage could well lead to major declines in marital disruption rates, even if no other characteristics relating to the youth were altered. The adjusted marital disruption rates for white women under the age of twenty are 19 percent, compared with 14 percent for those aged twenty to twenty-one, 12 percent for twenty-two- to twenty-three-year olds, and 9 percent for those women twenty-four years of age and older. Parallel declines are evidenced for black women.

After removing the effect of the other socioeconomic and demographic factors, the highest marital disruption probabilities are evidenced by women whose marriages are of intermediate length.[14] Apparently, separation and divorce are not so prevalent during the first two years of marriage as in the immediately subsequent years. As the marriage enters the fifth and sixth years, a pattern of decline in marital disruption probabilities appears, at least for this cohort of younger women.

From a demographic perspective, there is no evidence of any pattern of association between childbearing and marital disruption after controlling for related factors such as education, age, and duration of marriage. Thus the data suggest that it is not the presence or absence of a child per se that is concomitant with marital breakdown. Rather, other factors associated with the respondent and the marriage that are in turn determinants of childbearing are more likely to be the root causes.

As a final note, there is a definite independent positive association between the probability of a white woman's marital disruption and the ease with which one can obtain a divorce in a state. White respondents have about a 10 percent adjusted marital disruption probability in states where divorce rates are low, 14 percent where they are moderate, and a 21 percent adjusted probability in states where rates are the highest. Thus the data support the notion (for white women, at least) that institutional variations in divorce laws do play a major independent role in determining divorce levels.[15]

From an overall viewpoint, it seems that direct economic factors are of somewhat less importance as determinants of a marital breakdown than are other socioeconomic background and demographic factors. To the extent that the background factors are indirect determinants of income and other work-related factors, the case is obviously being overstated. However, in retrospect, the results should not be surprising. If men and women marry largely for noneconomic reasons, it is not inconsistent that large proportions of dissolving marriages should similarly have noneconomic motivations.

## The Socioeconomic Consequences of Marital Disruption

The short-term social and economic consequences of a marital disruption are visibly manifested in a number of ways. The focus of this section is on measuring the extent to which a woman is financially disadvantaged by the loss of her husband's income, the ways in which she seeks to alleviate this disadvantage, and how successful she is in doing so.

### The Transition Process: The Income Factor

From an economic perspective, changes in family income levels represent perhaps the most overt manifestation of disadvantage associated with marital disruption. While the numbers vary considerably, depending on whether one uses median or mean income estimates, the basic patterns depicted are similar.[16] An examination of table 7-3 indicates clearly the sharp decline in family income associated with the marital disruption process. When one analyzes the changes in family income, it becomes evident that all of the decline reflects the loss of the husband's income, primarily his earnings. Also, from a total family income perspective, one can see that the woman's earnings show an increase between the pre- and postdisruption periods, thus compensating to varying degrees for the loss of the husband's income.

For whites between time $T$ and $T + 2$ there is an overall decline of $2,990 (in 1967 dollars) in total income less respondent's earnings. This decline is partially compensated for by an increase of $1,420 in the respondent's earnings. Thus the white woman has compensated for 47 percent of the income loss

**Table 7-3**

**Mean Income Characteristics of Respondents Experiencing a Marital Disruption at Time $T$, $T + 1$, and $T + 2$, by Race[a]**

| Mean Income Characteristics | Whites | | | Blacks | | |
|---|---|---|---|---|---|---|
| | $T$ | $T + 1$ | $T + 2$ | $T$ | $T + 1$ | $T + 2$ |
| Mean family income | 7,552 | 5,197 | 5,983 | 6,251 | 3,967 | 3,794 |
| Mean family income less respondent's earnings | 5,845 | 2,709 | 2,855 | 4,658 | 2,344 | 1,756 |
| Mean respondent's earnings | 1,708 | 2,489 | 3,128 | 1,594 | 1,622 | 2,037 |
| Mean per capita income per family member | 2,688 | 2,124 | 2,656 | 1,721 | 1,176 | 1,024 |
| Mean family size | 2.8 | 2.4 | 2.3 | 3.6 | 3.4 | 3.7 |
| Number of respondents | 229 | 232 | 126 | 166 | 173 | 106 |

[a]Data for $T + 1$ and $T + 2$ are limited to those marital disruptees who have not remarried or reconciled with their husbands as of those points in time. All income and earnings estimates are in 1967 dollars.

through increases in her work activity. For blacks, the analogous numbers are −$2,902 and +$443, so the average black woman replaces only 15 percent of the income loss.

While the rather sharp contrast between whites and blacks suggested by the preceding numbers accurately depicts the relative positions of white and black women, from the perspective of individuals within the family, it is perhaps more meaningful to analyze the foregoing income changes in per-capita terms. If one adjusts for changes in family size between the two points in time ($T$ to $T + 2$), per-capita income for blacks declines from $1,721 to $1,024, while there is no significant change in per-capita income in the white families. From a per-capita perspective, the white woman, by increasing both her own earnings and her access to other sources of unearned income, largely replaces the loss of her husband's earnings.[17] Of course, while her family per-capita earnings may be up to their previous level, the larger average child care and other associated costs (reflecting in part the need for many of the women to enter the labor force) may well leave her in worse financial condition than she had been prior to the disruption.[18] Also note that part of the white woman's ability to maintain her family's per-capita income reflects the sharp decline in the mean white-family size (reflecting the loss of the husband). The black woman is more likely to be joined by or to form into a family network after the disruption. This extended family certainly alleviates many of the social traumas associated with the marital disruption, but apparently is unable to augment the family income to any significant extent.

Public assistance represents another financial option available to the maritally disrupted woman. Table 7-4 shows that regardless of income level, families

**Table 7-4**

**Percentages of Marital Disruption and Reference Groups Receiving Welfare, by Race and Selected Income Characteristics at $T$, $T + 1$, and $T + 2$[a]**

| Selected Income Characteristics | Whites | | Blacks | |
|---|---|---|---|---|
| | Marital Disruptees | Reference Group | Marital Disruptees | Reference Group |
| All respondents | | | | |
| $T$ | 5.4 | 2.5 | 17.3 | 7.7 |
| $T + 1$ | 23.3 | 2.9 | 44.0 | 5.5 |
| $T + 2$ | 26.9 | 2.9 | 52.4 | 7.9 |
| Family income under $4000 | | | | |
| $T$ | 19.1 | 9.7 | 40.2 | 13.5 |
| $T + 1$ | 38.6 | 14.8 | 63.5 | 16.1 |
| $T + 2$ | 48.2 | 16.3 | 69.1 | 26.4 |
| All respondents with no earnings | | | | |
| $T$ | 9.2 | 4.9 | 30.1 | 12.2 |
| $T + 1$ | 48.3 | 5.1 | 77.5 | 10.5 |
| $T + 2$ | 69.3 | 4.6 | 94.2 | 13.3 |
| All respondents with earnings | | | | |
| $T$ | 3.7 | 1.5 | 12.9 | 6.0 |
| $T + 1$ | 17.0 | 1.6 | 30.7 | 3.2 |
| $T + 2$ | 18.5 | 1.5 | 40.7 | 5.6 |

[a]Data at $T + 1$ and $T + 2$ limited to marital disruptees who have not remarried or reconciled with their husbands as of those points in time. "Receiving welfare" reflects a positive response to the question, "Did anyone in this family receive any welfare or public assistance in the past twelve months?"

that either are *or will become* disrupted are more likely to be receiving some form of welfare transfer payment than similar "reference" families.[19] Also, in all instances, black families are more likely than white families to be receiving some form of public assistance. Regardless of race or income level, the proportion of maritally disrupted families receiving some form of assistance increases sharply as one moves from point $T$ to $T + 1$ to $T + 2$. The increasing proportions receiving some form of welfare are generally consistent with the earlier documented sharp declines in the family's earned income following the disruption event. Also, the racial variations can be at least partially explained by differences in earnings and the number of own children present in the year following the disruption.

## Changes in Labor Force Participation Levels

The preceding data suggest that employment is one major means by which women whose marriages disintegrate compensate for the loss of husbands' earnings. Figure 7-1 indicates the trend of participation levels between time $T-1$ and $T+2$ for black and white maritally disrupted women with and without children. For black and white women without children, labor force participation levels rapidly approach (and for white women, surpass) the labor force participation levels of never-married women at approximately the same ages. The participation levels for women with children show large increases, but these levels predictably remain well below those of their childless counterparts.[20]

At time $T$ about 12 percent of white and 29 percent of black disruptees in the labor force were unable to find jobs (table 7-1). Whites, regardless of their work status prior to the marital disruption, were more likely to be employed at

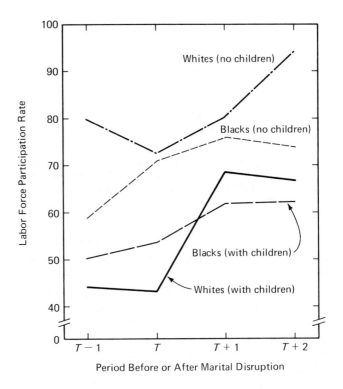

Note: Data for $T+1$ and $T+2$ are limited to marital disruptees who have not remarried or reconciled with spouse.

**Figure 7-1.** Labor Force Participation Rate of Respondents Experiencing a Marital Disruption at $T-1$, $T$, $T+1$, and $T+2$ by Race and Presence of Children

$T+1$ than were blacks. In particular, blacks in the labor force at $T$ apparently had much greater difficulty in maintaining that labor force attachment than comparable white workers.

To examine more carefully whether the prospective marital disruption event is associated with labor force participation levels *prior* to the disruption, independent of all other factors, a multivariate analysis was performed using labor force participation at time $T$ as the dependent variable. This labor supply model included the standard explanatory variables and, in addition, a variable indicating whether the women would have a marital disruption during the following year. White women whose marriages were to break up during the following year were indeed significantly more likely to be in the labor force. During the survey week before the marital disruption, their adjusted labor force participation rate was 62 percent compared with 55 percent for their nondisrupting counterparts. There were no significant differences, however, between the two black groups. Thus for white women at least, there is some evidence that anticipatory labor force behavior may be occurring—that is, some women in anticipation of a forthcoming marital breakup may be entering the labor force. These results are also consistent with our earlier hypothesized independence effect, whereby women with a closer attachment to the labor force would be expected to have higher marital disruption probabilities.[21]

It is also useful to compare the labor force transition between $T$ and $T+1$ for the reference group and the marital disruptees who were not in the labor force at $T$. About 56 percent of the white marital disruptees who were not in the labor force at $T$ were either employed or unemployed at $T+1$, compared with 23 percent for the comparable reference group. The corresponding percentages for the blacks were 48 and 30 percent, respectively.

Overall, about 81 percent of those marital disruptees employed at $T+1$ were working full time—at least thirty-five hours per week. This figure compares with only 68 percent for those in the reference group who were employed at the same point. Thus the greater need for income by the average marital disruptee is translated not only into higher levels of labor force participation but also into a lengthier work week. This result is particularly interesting, given that the average maritally disrupted woman is more likely to have children than the comparable woman still in an intact marriage. Indeed, 83 percent of the black and 61 percent of the white marital disruptees had at least one child in their household at $T$, compared with 68 percent for the black and 49 percent for the white reference group.

When this higher labor force participation pattern is combined with the knowledge that almost half of the maritally disrupted women had no other adult living in their household potentially available for child care and clearly had very limited funds for outside child-care assistance, the ability of these women to maintain employment continuity is quite remarkable. In any event, the employment needs of these women combined with their limited access to free child-care services and limited funds suggest that this group should receive the highest priority for child care and other forms of economic assistance.

*Work and Training*

Data from the NLS indicate that rather substantial numbers of women are enrolled in training programs of some kind in the periods immediately preceding and following the marital disruption event.[22] In addition, the proportion of white women enrolled in training during the preceding year increases rather sharply between $T$ and $T + 1$—from 16 to 26 percent. There is no corresponding increase for black women, although they exhibit an increase in training participation rates from 11 to 20 percent between $T + 1$ and $T + 2$. Thus whatever the reason for this difference, whites are better able to gain access to training programs when they need them. On the other hand, increased black participation in training associated with marital disruption is somewhat delayed, perhaps reflecting a lesser awareness of program availability and a greater need to seek immediate gainful employment.

Supplementary multivariate analysis of the determinants of training at time $T + 1$ for black and white marital disruptees indicates one other major variation between the two racial groups. White trainees are clearly selected out from the most educated of the eligibles, whereas blacks with the least education are more likely to be involved in training programs. Thus while maritally disrupted blacks may be less likely to move into training programs at that point in the life cycle, those who do enroll (from a positive perspective) are most in need of vocational assistance.

Since there are obvious associations between training and work at a given point in time, it is useful to inquire whether receipt of training between $T - 1$ and $T$ for those not in the labor force at $T$ is related to employment status at $T + 1$. Such training is associated with a higher probability of being employed at $T + 1$, with a lower unemployment rate, and with higher earnings. These patterns are in evidence for both black and white women, but should be interpreted cautiously because of the small sample size for the group that had previous training.

**Summary and Conclusions**

Whereas economic motives may be of only moderate importance as precipitating factors in a marital breakdown, economic consequences are very pronounced in the postdisruption life-cycle phase. Marital disruption is accompanied by sharp declines in family income, increased receipt of welfare, increased desire for job-related training, and higher labor force participation rates. Increased usage of income-maintenance programs occurs for large proportions of women, particularly black women with children, low education, few job skills, and outside financial resources.

The large proportion of all young adult couples who experience marital disruption and the substantial economic impact that this experience has on young women suggests that some thought should be given to developing a program of transition assistance for maritally disrupted women and their children. Such a program might include job guidance, training, day care for children, and temporary income maintenance.

## Notes

1. Alexander A. Plateris, "100 Years of Marriage and Divorce Statistics," *Vital and Health Statistics*, series 21, no. 24 (Washington, D.C.: Division of Vital Statistics, National Center for Health Statistics, 1973).

2. National Center for Health Statistics, "Final Divorce Statistics, 1975," *Monthly Vital Statistics Report*, vol. 26, no. 2–supplement 2 (Washington, D.C.: U.S. Department of Health, Education and Welfare, May 19, 1977).

3. U.S. Bureau of the Census, "Number, Timing, and Duration of Marriage: June 1975," *Current Population Reports* 23 (12) (Washington, D.C.: U.S. Government Printing Office, June 1975).

4. There are 520 women who can be identified as having had a first marital disruption at some time during the five-year period. All of these women were either already married in 1968 or married at some time after that point but before the 1973 interview (see appendix 7A for details concerning the "eligible for disruption" population). Of the 520 women, 38 are excluded from the analysis because they moved from a "never married" status in one survey to a "maritally disrupted" status in the next, and no information exists with respect to the characteristics of their husbands. Thirty-eight cases are also excluded because the respondents were enrolled in school at the last survey date prior to their marital disruption, which makes information on their predisruption labor market activity and earnings less meaningful. The sample of disruptees used in the analysis numbers 449 (264 whites and 185 blacks).

Note that women whose marital status was "separated" or "divorced" at the time of the first interview are excluded from the analysis, since we cannot specify when the disruption occurred or the characteristics of the women and their families in the predisruption period.

There are two types of cases that prevent the criteria for inclusion in our sample of marital disruptees from being applied with complete precision. First, women who separate and return to the *same husband* between two survey dates cannot be identified. Second, if a woman experienced a marital disruption prior to the 1968 interview but was once again in a "married, husband present" status as of 1968, she would not be identifiable as a marital disruptee. To the extent that either of these cases exist, the women in question are classified among the nondisruptees.

5. Since many women were eligible to be in the reference group at more than one survey date, the eligible respondents were randomly distributed across survey years in the same proportions as the disruptees were distributed. Further adjustments were made in the reference group consistent with the adjustment made in the marital disruptee population that excluded women who were never married at $T$ but were maritally disrupted by $T + 1$. See appendix 7A for details.

6. For discussions concerning the separate and interacting effects of social status and education see, for example, Hugh Carter and Paul C. Glick, *Marriage and Divorce: A Social and Economic Study* (Cambridge: Harvard University Press, 1970); Larry L. Bumpass and James A. Sweet, "Background and Early Marital Factors in Marital Disruption," CDE Working Paper 75-31 (Madison: Center for Demography and Ecology, University of Wisconsin, 1975); and Phillips Cutright, "Income and Family Events: Marital Stability," *Journal of Marriage and the Family* (March 1971):307-317. For a review of the literature on intergenerational instability see Hallowell Pope and Charles W. Mueller, "The Intergenerational Transmission of Marital Instability," *Journal of Social Issues* 32 (1976):49-66.

7. For example, see Paul C. Glick and Arthur J. Norton, "Frequency, Duration and Probability of Marriage and Divorce," *Journal of Marriage and the Family* (May 1971):307-317; and Frank F. Furstenberg, Jr., "Premarital Pregnancy and Marital Instability," *Journal of Social Issues* 32 (Winter 1976):67-86.

8. For example, see Cutright, "Income and Family Events"; Gary S. Becker, Elisabeth M. Landes, and Robert T. Michael, "An Economic Analysis of Marital Instability," *Journal of Political Economy* 85 (December 1977):1141-1187; Heather Ross and Isabel Sawhill, *Time of Transition* (Washington, D.C.: The Urban Institute, 1975); and Andrew Cherlin, "Economics, Social Roles, and Marital Separations." Preliminary draft. Johns Hopkins University, 1976.

9. Ross and Sawhill, *Time of Transition.*

10. Cherlin, "Economics, Social Roles, and Marital Separations."

11. Ross and Sawhill, *Time of Transition.*

12. Ibid.

13. Actual hourly earnings are hypothesized to be a function of the respondent's education, work experience, southern/nonsouthern residence, SMSA/non-SMSA residence, and job tenure. From these estimates for women who were working, we then estimated values for nonworkers, assuming them to have similar wage structures. While there obviously is a certain built-in collinearity between potential wage and educational attainment, and since education is an input into the wage equation, the inclusion of both in the same model in no major way alters the results. Appendix 7A gives a detailed description of the construction of the wage variable.

14. The disruption probabilities for the newly married group are slightly artificially depressed since those women who are never married at time $T$ but maritally disrupted by time $T + 1$ are excluded from the model. However, even when these women are included, their disruption rates are significantly below those whose marriages were of an intermediate length.

15. This variation in disruption probabilities by state divorce rates may be seen to be independent of urban-rural variations among states since a control for this factor is included in the model. Note that white individuals living in metropolitan areas are significantly more likely than individuals living in rural areas to have their marriages disrupted. While acknowledging a certain circularity between state divorce rates and marital disruption probabilities, we feel that the use of the variable is justified as representing (at least partially) differential access to divorce. This is because many of the individual characteristics that might otherwise affect variations in divorce probabilities are already controlled for in the model.

16. The skewness of the income and earnings distributions results in major discrepancies between the median and mean earnings and income estimates. A relatively small number of high-income individuals or families can significantly raise mean levels without altering medians. This is particularly true when one is focusing on a group where a large proportion is at low-income levels. Median earnings estimates have certain advantages when analyzing data for lower income groups since the "median" estimates more closely approximate earnings for the average individual. However, mean estimates are more functional when one wishes to examine the components of the income, since the mean components are by definition additive, whereas the median components need not add to the total. For this reason, mean estimates are used in this study where components of income are being examined, and medians are used where only overall comparisons are being made.

17. A cautionary note regarding these racial differences in income is in order. To the extent that welfare payments and/or income from "other" family members may represent more important income sources in maritally disrupted black households, differences between black and white incomes may be overstated due to the possible understatement of these two income sources.

18. To the extent that white women are more likely to use more family child-care sources and thus have higher child-care costs on the average than black women, the preceding statistics may overstate somewhat the per-capita income differences between black and white families. See Richard Shortlidge and Patricia Brito, *How Women Arrange for the Care of Their Children While They Work: A Study of Child Care Arrangements, Costs, and Preferences in 1971* (Columbus: The Ohio State University, Center for Human Resource Research, 1977).

19. The survey questions asked with regard to receipt of public assistance do not discriminate as to the type of transfer payment received or which member of the family is receiving the assistance.

20. Although the direction of causality is unclear, if the samples of white and black women are stratified by the receipt or nonreceipt of public assistance, the racial difference in postdisruption labor force participation rates is virtually eliminated.

21. Frank L. Mott and Sylvia F. Moore, "The Dynamics of Marital Disruption: Determinants and Consequences." Paper presented at the Population Association Meetings, St. Louis, Missouri, April 1977.

22. The following question was asked of women not enrolled in school: "Since this time last year have you taken any training courses or education programs of any kind either on the job or elsewhere?"

# Appendix 7A:
# Construction of the
# Marital Disruption and
# Reference Group
# Samples and the
# Independent Variables

## Construction of the Marital Disruption and Reference Group Samples

### The Marital Disruption Sample

All young women who divorce or separate for the first time during the 1968 to 1973 period are defined as the marital disruption sample. A "maritally disrupted" woman will only be counted once—the year within the 1968 to 1973 period when she first appears as maritally disrupted (separated or divorced)—that is, if a woman were married with her spouse present in 1968, separated in 1969, and divorced in 1970, she would appear in the numerator of the marital disruption variable in 1969 but not again in 1970.

The following slippage exists in being able to properly identify all disrupting women:

1. Women who were divorced or separated at some point before the first survey in 1968 cannot be identified.

2. Women who are married with the same husband present in successive years and who had a separation in the intervening interval cannot be identified.

In general, all other women who either separate or divorce between 1968 and 1973 can be identified unless, of course, they leave the sample before the marital disruption event.

### The Reference Group

Whereas a first marital disruption represents a unique event, appearing in the (maritally stable) reference group is not, since many women obviously are "eligible to have a marital disruption" in more than one survey year. Thus to count a woman in the reference group every year she is eligible to have a marital disruption would result in massive double counting. For this reason, we have used the following procedure for defining that group:

1. Every woman who is "eligible" at some point between 1968 and 1973 is included in the reference group only one time.

2. After excluding those women who are known to experience a marital

133

134

disruption between 1968 and 1973, the remainder are randomly distributed across the survey years roughly in proportion to the distribution of marital disruption over the five-year period—that is, if $x$ percent of all the first marital disruptions occurred between 1968 and 1969, then $x$ percent of the eligible reference group was randomly assigned to that interval. Thus once an individual is selected for the reference group in a given year, she is no longer eligible for inclusion in any other year.

The preceding should meet the basic objectives of a properly defined reference group—that is, it (1) defines women who were eligible to have a marital disruption but did not do so during the appropriate time period, and (2) assures that the reference group is demographically and temporally appropriate.

Variables for this reference group are generally measured in the year that the particular individual is selected to appear. For example, if we select a woman for our reference group in 1970, her socioeconomic characteristics (as entered in our model) will be measured as of the 1970 interview. The only exception is the case of those who were never married in the year in which they were selected to appear. The socioeconomic characteristics of these women will be measured as of the next interview, when they are married. A more detailed description of the variables discussed in the following section as well as descriptions of other variables used in this chapter are available from the authors.

## Construction of Independent Variables

### Accessibility of Welfare in State

To measure the ease of obtaining benefits, we use the proportion of potentially eligible households (according to census definition) actually receiving AFDC assistance by state. The actual benefit level received is proxied by Social Security statistics giving average payment per recipient by state. We can then construct a variable of the following form:

1. High accessibility - high benefits
2. High accessibility - low benefits
   Low accessibility - high benefits } ("other")
3. Low accessibility - low benefits

High accessibility means that the state has above the mean proportion of potentially eligible households actually receiving AFDC. High benefit levels mean that the state has above the mean average payment per recipient.

### Ease of Divorce: Divorce Rate in State

The divorce rate by state of residence is used to proxy for the ease of obtaining a divorce in a given state.

1. 0-2.6 divorce rate per 1,000 population
2. 2.7-4.1 divorce rate per 1,000
3. 4.2-6.7 divorce rate per 1,000
4. 6.8 or higher divorce rate per 1,000
5. State of residence unknown

*Potential Wage*

Actual hourly earnings are hypothesized to be a function of the respondent's education, work experience, southern/nonsouthern residence, SMSA/non-SMSA residence, and job tenure. From these estimates, assuming women with like characteristics will have similar labor supply behavior, a potential wage is estimated. The potential wage is standardized in 1967 dollars and computed regardless of whether the woman is presently in the labor market.

For whites, the wage equation is as follows (with $t$ statistics in parentheses):

$$\text{Wage} = \underset{(2.95)}{140.54} - \underset{(-2.83)}{20.873} \times (\text{Education}) + \underset{(6.52)}{15.566} \times (\text{Work Experience})$$

$$+ \underset{(4.42)}{14.703} \times (\text{Job Tenure}) - \underset{(-2.90)}{1.2874} \times (\text{Job Tenure}^2)$$

$$- \underset{(-3.04)}{0.69706} \times (\text{Work Experience}^2) + \underset{(5.28)}{25.870} \times (\text{SMSA})$$

$$- \underset{(-0.98)}{4.9788} \times (\text{South}) + \underset{(5.59)}{1.6068} \times (\text{Education}^2)$$

For blacks, the wage equation is as follows (with $t$ statistics in parentheses):

$$\text{Wage} = \underset{(3.77)}{193.79} - \underset{(-2.49)}{20.904} \times (\text{Education}) + \underset{(5.25)}{14.012} \times (\text{Work Experience})$$

$$+ \underset{(2.10)}{8.8415} \times (\text{Job Tenure}) - \underset{(-0.58)}{0.35380} \times (\text{Job Tenure}^2)$$

$$- \underset{(-4.54)}{1.1459} \times (\text{Work Experience}^2) + \underset{(3.31)}{20.261} \times (\text{SMSA})$$

$$- \underset{(-7.17)}{39.102} \times (\text{South}) + \underset{(4.13)}{1.4513} \times (\text{Education}^2)$$

# 8

## Highlights of the Volume and Some Policy Implications

*Frank L. Mott*

The research presented in this volume focuses, directly and indirectly, on questions associated with the prospective lifetime work activities of women who are in their early adult years. It is clear that a substantial proportion of all such women, for varying reasons, will spend a major part of their lives in the labor force. This volume considers several factors associated with this trend including the educational and training experiences of women now reaching adulthood, rationales associated with work attachment during the early years of marriage, and the implications of marital breakdown and of family mobility patterns for work and career.

In several important ways, the potential quality of the lifetime work experience is contingent on the respondent's background. Not only do parental factors directly affect the quantity and quality of a young woman's educational experiences (chapter 2), they also have a significant effect on the type of career path a woman plans to follow (chapter 4). In addition, the direct impact of parents on a daughter's educational desires, expectations, and actual experiences will ultimately alter both the quantity and quality of her adult work behavior.

We have found, not unexpectedly, that social-class background, particularly parental income, is a powerful determinant of the likelihood of college attendance. This social-class factor operates by affecting a youth's educational desires and, more directly, by determining at least partially her ability to afford college.

Whereas this conclusion is perhaps not surprising, what is of more than academic interest is the rather striking fact that the lesser likelihood of black youth to desire and actually attend college can be fully explained by the different socioeconomic characteristics of the two racial groups. In other words, a black young woman with socioeconomic background characteristics similar to the average white youth is, if anything, *more* likely to desire to attend and actually attend college.

As a corollary to this economic theme, there is evidence that the parental income factor becomes even more dominant as a predictor of college attendance during periods of high unemployment. Thus all the evidence in this volume is highly consistent with the thought that equality of education, particularly at the college level, might be furthered through income-subsidizing measures that would enable more students from low-income environments to attend college. This statement is relevant not only with regard to attendance per se, but equally with regard to a youth's ability to attend a college commensurate with her ability.

Moving from the dynamics of the educational attainment process into the early years of work attachment, the importance of socioeconomic factors continues to be evident. Whereas virtually all women work at some point after leaving school but before the birth of their first child, major racial and socioeconomic differences begin to appear as the birth event approaches (chapter 3). First, black young women, particularly the better educated, are much more likely than white women to be out of the labor force for only a short time in connection with the birth of their first child. In addition, the black woman not only returns to the work force more quickly but is much more likely to seek full-time employment when she does return. Indeed, over 80 percent of the black women who return to the labor force ultimately work at least thirty-five hours a week. This is as high a proportion working full time as before the birth. Also, for both black and white women who return to the labor force, the better educated are much better able to improve on the wages of their prebirth job.

We have already noted that, if given the option, black women will seek more education. This education, in turn, enhances their ability not only to maintain closer ties with the work force but to enjoy superior occupational status and remuneration. Indeed, there is clear evidence of a selectivity process: women capable of earning higher salaries in the labor market are more likely to maintain their work ties. Conversely, women with the least economic bargaining power—the less educated and skilled—are least likely to find and maintain employment at a reasonable wage level.

While it is evident that a substantial proportion of all women plan to have extensive ties with the labor market, the research reported in chapter 4 indicates that there still are extensive labor market information lags that impede appropriate career decisions. In general, when queried about their occupational plans for age thirty-five, young women tended to mention only a limited number of occupations, most of which are jobs that have been traditionally held by women. Thus it appears that the women's liberation movement has not yet made significant inroads into the career thinking of young women. Moreover, some of these traditionally female occupations represent economically irrational choices under existing circumstances. For example, among the college educated, about one-third of the white women and almost a quarter of the black plan to be in a teaching profession by the time they reach age thirty-five. This is an occupational area that currently does not offer the best job prospects. There is, however, some cause for optimism in this regard; between 1968 and 1973 there were decreases in the proportions planning to enter teaching as a career, perhaps reflecting a salutary effect of maturation on a young woman's sophistication about the world of work. On the other hand, many of the "high-growth" occupations chosen by young women are in the health field, where a disproportionate number of the jobs for college graduates are at relatively low salary levels.

That women are to a greater degree planning more extensive commitments to the labor force than had been true in the past has major implications, some of which are highlighted in chapter 5. One may expect that young women will display a greater willingness to accept occupational training for general as well as specific job skills even at the cost of lower initial wages. In other words, there is evidence that women with stronger prospective attachments to the labor force are more willing to accept lower initial wages as a price they must pay for a current job providing training and thereby promising higher lifetime earnings.

Parenthetically, it is useful to speculate about the possible impact of this increasing level of work activity among young women for the work prospects of subsequent generations. To the extent that we are now witnessing a secular change in the likely lifetime work patterns of women, supply and demand patterns for specific occupations may be different in the future than they have been in the past. For example, most women have traditionally withdrawn from the labor force during the family formative years, sometimes returning for a "second career" as their youngest child ages. These traditional patterns of labor force participation opened up many job slots for new graduates in an occupation like teaching. To the extent that the current generation of women will no longer interrupt their careers when children are born, jobs available for new entrants into the labor market will become more limited. In times of high unemployment, as at present, this situation is likely to be exacerbated for women will have a greater tendency to "hang on" to their jobs in the justified fear that if they quit they would have a more difficult time when seeking to return to work.

While the teaching profession is admittedly a rather extreme illustration of this phenomenon, many other occupations, even those with relatively strong growth potential, could have been cited. The fundamental point is that, at least for the transition generation, major changes in women's labor force withdrawal patterns may well be closely associated with greater labor force entry problems and concomitantly, higher levels of youth unemployment. Within this context, it is useful to emphasize once more the lesson to be learned from chapter 4; career guidance must make women aware of a broader range of possible jobs and careers than has traditionally been the case. This would increase the flexibility of young women in seeking jobs or formulating career ideas during a period when many of the traditional avenues of employment offer only limited prospects for success.

Two other major events in the lives of many young adult women—migration and marital disruption—also have major implications for their labor force behavior. Chapter 6 highlights the major negative impact that the family migration decision can have on both the wife's attachment to the labor force as well as her annual earnings. The research suggests that migration not only reduces the wife's earnings on the average but, as a direct result of this reduction, reduces total family earnings as well. In other words, the increased earnings of the husband that accompany migration do not, on the average, compensate for the loss of earnings of the wife. From a purely economic perspective one might thus question the desirability of many moves. However, the results are consistent with the idea that economics may well *not* be the major motivating force behind many families' moves—at least in the short run.

Whereas migration tends to be associated with reduced levels of work attachment, chapter 7 shows clearly that the process of marital disruption generally increases attachments to the work force, particularly for white women. Thus the ability to find meaningful employment enables women at least partially to compensate for the loss of a husband's earnings. The results suggest that white women are able to compensate for almost half of their husbands' earnings loss through employment after disruption. The corresponding statistic for black women is only about 15 percent. Partly as a result of this increase in earnings, white-family income after the marital disruption (on a per-capita basis) rapidly approaches predisruption levels. This recovery is not apparent for black families. Job-related training, to which white women also apparently have greater access, contributes to this ability to cope economically, as women who receive training in the year immediately preceding a marital disruption tend to have higher earnings as well as lower levels of unemployment in the year following the marital disruption event.

As noted earlier, work discontinuities associated with child birth tend increasingly to be brief. Work discontinuities and entry patterns associated with migration and marital disruption are two additional phenomena that affect large numbers of women and are associated with a desire and need for remunerative employment. What should be readily apparent is that, whereas most young adult women work, they also commonly encounter life-cycle events requiring at least a brief interruption in employment. Moreover, many of these women wish the discontinuity to be brief. The more effective the guidance, training, and other work-related information young women (especially those with limited formal education) receive, the greater the likelihood that the actual pattern of work interruptions will match their needs and desires.

Unfortunately, most young women of high-school age are relatively unaware of what the future holds in store for them, both in regard to their likely work activity as well as the frequent and not atypical pattern of work interruption. To fail to make this clear to the current generation of young women approaching adulthood is to do a disservice both to them and to society. The adolescent woman must be encouraged to acquire job-related skills that will serve her for a lifetime of work activity.

# Appendix

# Appendix:
# Sampling,
# Interviewing, and
# Estimating Procedures

The Survey of Work Experience of Young Women is one of the four longitudinal surveys sponsored by the Employment and Training Administration of the U.S. Department of Labor. Taken together, these four surveys constitute the National Longitudinal Surveys (NLS). Each of the four NLS samples was designed by the Bureau of the Census to represent the civilian noninstitutional population of the United States at approximately the time of the initial survey. Because of attrition from the samples over the years of the surveys, they cannot be construed to be precisely representative of the civilian noninstitutional population in any year after the first.

## Sample Design

The cohort is represented by a multistage probability sample located in 235 sample areas comprising 485 counties and independent cities representing every state and the District of Columbia. The 235 sample areas were selected by grouping all of the nation's counties and independent cities into about 1,900 primary sampling units (PSUs), and further forming 235 strata of one or more PSUs that were relatively homogeneous according to socioeconomic characteristics. Within each of the strata a single PSU was selected to represent the stratum. Within each PSU a probability sample of housing units was selected to represent the civilian noninstitutional population.

Since one of the survey requirements was to provide separate reliable statistics for blacks, households in predominantly black enumeration districts (EDs) were selected at a rate approximately three times that for households in predominantly white EDs. The sample was designed to provide approximately 5,000 respondents—about 1,500 blacks and 3,500 whites.

An initial sample of about 42,000 housing units was selected, and a screening interview took place in March and April 1966. Of this number, about 7,500 units were found to be vacant, occupied by persons whose usual residence was elsewhere, changed from residential use, or demolished. On the other hand, about 900 additional units were found that had been created within existing living space or had been changed from what was previously nonresidential space. Thus, 35,360 housing units were available for interview, of which usable information was collected for 34,622 households, a completion rate of 98.0 percent.

143

Following the initial interview and screening operation, the sample was rescreened in the fall of 1966, immediately prior to the first Survey of Work Experience of Males aged fourteen to twenty-four. For the rescreening operation, the sample was stratified by the presence or absence of a fourteen- to twenty-four-year-old woman in the household. The rescreened sample was used to designate 5,533 young women aged fourteen to twenty-four as of January 1, 1968, to be interviewed for the Survey of Work Experience. These were sampled differentially within four strata: whites in white EDs (that is, EDs that contained predominantly white households); nonwhites in white EDs; whites in nonwhite EDs; and nonwhites in nonwhite EDs.

## The Field Work

Over 300 interviewers were assigned to each of the surveys. Preference in the selection of interviewers was given to those who had experience on one of the other longitudinal surveys. Since many of the procedures and the labor force and socioeconomic concepts used in this survey were similar to those used in the Current Population Survey (CPS), the Bureau of the Census used interviewers with CPS experience whenever possible.

Training for the interviewers consisted of a home-study package that included a reference manual explaining the purpose, procedures, and concepts used in the survey and the home-study exercises, and a set of questions based on points explained in the manual. In addition to the home-study package, there were one-day classroom training sessions in the early survey years that all interviewers were required to attend. All training materials were prepared by the Census Bureau staff and reviewed by the Employment and Training Administration and the Center for Human Resource Research of The Ohio State University. Professional members of the participating organizations observed both the training sessions and the actual interviewing.

In addition to training, a field edit was instituted to ensure adequate quality. This consisted of a full edit of the completed questionnaires by data collection center staffs. The edit consisted of reviewing each questionnaire from beginning to end to determine whether the entries were complete and consistent and whether the skip instructions were being followed. If there were minor problems, the interviewer was contacted by phone, told of the error, and asked to contact the respondent for further clarification. For more serious problems, the interviewer was retrained, either totally or in part, and the questionnaire was returned to her for completion.

## Estimating Methods

The estimating procedure used in the NLS involved multistage ratio estimates.

*Basic Weight*

The first step was the assignment to each sample case of a basic weight consisting of the reciprocal of the final probability of selection. The probability reflects the differential sampling that was employed by race within each stratum.

*Noninterview Adjustment*

In the initial survey the weights for all those interviewed were adjusted to the extent needed to account for persons for whom no information was obtained because of absence, refusal, or unavailability for other reasons. This adjustment was made separately for the following groupings: census region, place of residence, and race.

*Ratio Estimates*

The distribution of the population selected for the sample may differ somewhat, by chance, from that of the nation as a whole with respect to residence, age, race, and sex. Since these population characteristics are closely correlated with the principal measurements made from the sample, the measurements can be substantially improved when weighted appropriately to conform to the known distribution of these population characteristics.[1] This was accomplished in the initial survey through two stages of ratio estimation.

The first stage of ratio estimation takes into account differences at the time of the 1960 Census in the distribution by race and residence of the population as estimated from the sample PSUs, and that of the total population in each of the four major regions of the country. Using 1960 Census data, estimated population totals by race and residence for each region were computed by appropriately weighting the census counts for PSUs in the sample. Ratios were then computed between these estimates (based on sample PSUs) and the actual population totals for the region as shown by the 1960 Census.

In the second stage, the sample proportions were adjusted to independent current estimates of the civilian noninstitutionalized population by age and race. These estimates were prepared by carrying forward the most recent census data (1960) to take account of subsequent aging of the population, mortality, and migration between the United States and other countries.[2] The adjustment was made by race within four age groupings.

*Weights for Subsequent Years*

As a result of the preceding steps, each sample person has a weight that remains unchanged throughout the life of the study. The universe of study was thus fixed at the time of interview for the first survey. Since no reweighting of the sample was made after subsequent surveys, the group of interviewed persons is an unbiased sample of the population group in existence at the time of the first survey only. The number of young women with whom initial interviews were conducted was 5,159.

## Coding and Editing

Most of the data on the interview schedules required no coding, since a majority of the answers were numerical entries or in the form of precoded categories. However, clerical coding was necessary for the occupational and industrial classification of the several jobs referred to in the interview. The Census Bureau's standard occupation and industry codes used for the CPS were employed for this purpose. Codes for other open-ended questions were assigned by the Census Bureau, in some cases on the basis of guidelines developed by the Center for Human Resource Research from tallies of subsamples of the returns.

The consistency edits for the interview schedules were completed on the computer by the Census Bureau. For the parts of the questionnaire that were similar to the CPS, a modified CPS edit was used. For all other sections, separate consistency checks were performed. None of the edits included an allocation routine that was dependent on averages or random information from outside sources, since such allocated data could not be expected to be consistent with data from previous or subsequent surveys. However, where the answer to a question was obvious from others in the questionnaire, the missing answer was entered on the tape.

## Notes

1. For a more detailed explanation of the preparation of the estimates, see U.S. Bureau of the Census, Technical Paper no. 7, *The Current Population Survey—A Report on Methodology* (Washington, D.C.: U.S. Government Printing Office, 1963).

2. For a description of the methods used in preparing these independent population estimates, see U.S. Bureau of the Census, *Current Population Reports* Series P-25, no. 352, "Estimates of the Population of the United States by Age, Color, and Sex: July 1, 1966" (Washington, D.C.: U.S. Government Printing Office, November 18, 1966).

# Bibliography

Almquist, Elizabeth M. "Sex Stereotypes in Occupational Choice: The Case of College Women." *Journal of Vocational Behavior* 5 (August 1974), pp. 13-21.

Almquist, Elizabeth M., and Shirley S. Angrist. "Role Model Influences on College Women's Career Aspirations." *Merrill-Palmer Quarterly* 17 (July 1971), pp. 263-279.

Becker, Gary S. *Human Capital: A Theoretical and Empirical Analysis, with Special Reference to Education.* National Bureau of Economic Research. New York: Columbia University Press, 1964.

Becker, Gary S. *Human Capital and the Personal Distribution of Income: An Analytic Approach.* Woytinsky Lecture no. 1. Ann Arbor: Institute of Public Administration, University of Michigan, 1967.

Becker, Gary S. *The Economics of Discrimination*, 2nd ed. Chicago: University of Chicago Press, 1971.

Becker, Gary S., Elisabeth M. Landes, and Robert T. Michael. "An Economic Analysis of Marital Instability." *Journal of Political Economy* 85 (December 1977), pp. 1141-1187.

Blinder, Alan S. "Wage Discrimination: Reduced Form and Structural Estimates." *Journal of Human Resources* (Fall 1973), pp. 436-455.

Blinder, Alan S. "On Dogmatism in Human Capital Theory." *Journal of Human Resources* (Winter 1976), pp. 8-22.

Bowen, William G., and T. Aldrich Finegan. *The Economics of Labor Force Participation.* Princeton, N.J.: Princeton University Press, 1969.

Bowles, Samuel. "Migration as Investment: Empirical Tests of the Human Investment Approach to Geographical Mobility." *The Review of Economics and Statistics* 52 (November 1970), pp. 356-362.

Bumpass, Larry L., and James A. Sweet. "Background and Early Marital Factors in Marital Disruption." CDE Working Paper 75-31. Madison: Center for Demography and Ecology, University of Wisconsin, 1975.

Campbell, R., and B. Siegel. "The Demand for Higher Education in the United States 1919-1964." *American Economic Review* 57 (June 1967), pp. 482-494.

Carey, Max L. "Revised Occupational Projections to 1985." *Monthly Labor Review* 99 (November 1976), pp. 10-22.

Carnegie Commission on Higher Education. *College Graduates and Jobs.* New York: McGraw-Hill, 1973.

Carnegie Commission on Higher Education. *Opportunities for Women in Higher Education.* New York: McGraw-Hill, 1973.

Carter, Hugh, and Paul C. Glick. *Marriage and Divorce: A Social and Economic Study.* Cambridge: Harvard University Press, 1970.

Center for Human Resource Research. "The National Longitudinal Surveys Handbook." Mimeographed. Columbus: The Ohio State University, revised 1977.

Cherlin, Andrew. "Economics, Social Roles, and Marital Separations." Preliminary draft. Johns Hopkins University, 1976.

Chiswick, Barry, James Fachler, June O'Neill, and Solomon Polachek. "The Effect of Occupation on Race and Sex Differences in Hourly Earnings." *Public Data Use* 3 (April 1975), pp. 2-9.

Cutright, Phillips. "Income and Family Events: Marital Stability." *Journal of Marriage and the Family* (March 1971), pp. 307-317.

DaVanzo, Julie. *Why Families Move.* Washington, D.C.: U.S. Government Printing Office, 1977.

Eldridge, Hope T. "A Cohort Approach to the Analysis of Migration Differentials." *Demography* 1 (1964), pp. 212-219.

Fleisher, Belton M. "Mother's Home Time and the Production of Child Quality." *Demography* 14 (May 1977), pp. 197-212.

Fuchs, Victor. "A Note on Sex Segregation in Professional Occupation." *Explorations in Economic Research* 2 (Winter 1975), pp. 105-111.

Furstenberg, Frank F., Jr. "Premarital Pregnancy and Marital Instability." *Journal of Social Issues* 32 (Winter 1976), pp. 67-86.

Glick, Paul C., and Arthur J. Norton. "Frequency, Duration and Probability of Marriage and Divorce." *Journal of Marriage and the Family* (May 1971), pp. 307-317.

Goldberg, David. "The Fertility of Two Generation Urbanites." *Population Studies* (March 1959), pp. 214-222.

Goldstein, Sidney, and Calvin Goldscheider. *Jewish Americans.* Englewood Cliffs, N.J.: Prentice-Hall, 1968.

Harmon, Lenore W. "Anatomy of Career Commitment in Women." *Journal of Counseling Psychology* 17 (1970), pp. 77-80.

Hause, John C. "Earnings Profile: Ability and Schooling." *Journal of Political Economy* 80 (May/June 1972, part 2), pp. S108-138.

Hayghe, Howard. "Marital and Family Characteristics of the Labor Force in March 1973." *Monthly Labor Review* 97 (April 1974), pp. 21-27.

Hayghe, Howard. "Marital and Family Characteristics of the Labor Force, March 1975." *Monthly Labor Review* 98 (November 1975), pp. 52-55.

Hill, C. Russell, and Frank P. Stafford. "Allocation of Time to Preschool Children and Educational Opportunity." *Journal of Human Resources* 9 (Summer 1974), pp. 323-341.

Hoffer, Stefan N. "Private Rates of Return to Higher Education for Women." *Review of Economics and Statistics* 55 (November 1973), pp. 482-486.

Jerome, Harry. *Migration and Business Cycles.* New York: National Bureau of Economic Research, 1926.

Johnston, J. *Econometric Methods,* 2nd ed. New York: McGraw-Hill, 1972.

Jusenius, Carol L. "The Influence of Work Experience and Typicality of Occupational Assignment on Women's Earnings." In Herbert S. Parnes et al., *Dual Careers: A Longitudinal Analysis of the Labor Market Experience of Women*, vol. IV. Manpower Research Monograph no. 21. U.S. Department of Labor. Washington, D.C.: U.S. Government Printing Office, 1976, pp. 97-118.

Jusenius, Carol, and Steven H. Sandell. "Barriers to Entry and Re-entry into the Labor Force." Columbus: Center for Human Resource Research, The Ohio State University, June 1974.

Jusenius, Carol L., and Richard L. Shortlidge, Jr. *Dual Careers: A Longitudinal Study of the Labor Market Experience of Women*, vol. III. Manpower Research Monograph no. 21. U.S. Department of Labor. Washington, D.C.: U.S. Government Printing Office, 1975.

Klemmack, David L., and John N. Edwards. "Women's Acquisitions of Stereotyped Occupational Aspirations." *Sociology and Social Research* 57 (July 1973), pp. 510-525.

Kohen, Andrew, and Roger Roderick. "The Effects of Race and Sex Discrimination on Early-Career Earnings." Columbus, Center for Human Resource Research, The Ohio State University, 1975.

Lansing, John B., and Eva Mueller. *The Geographic Mobility of Labor*. Ann Arbor: Institute for Social Research, 1967.

Leibowitz, Arleen S. "Women's Allocation of Time to Market and Nonmarket Activities: Differences by Education." Ph.D. dissertation, Columbia University, 1972.

Leibowitz, Arleen S. "Education and Home Production." *American Economic Review* 64 (May 1974), pp. 243-250.

Long, Larry H. "Women's Labor Force Participation and the Residential Mobility of Families." *Social Forces* 52 (March 1974), pp. 342-349.

Lowry, Ira S. *Migration and Metropolitan Growth: Two Analytical Models*. San Francisco: Chandler Publishing Company, 1966.

Merton, Robert K. *Social Theory and Social Structure*. New York: The Free Press, 1968.

Mincer, Jacob. "The Distribution of Labor Incomes: A Survey with Special Reference to the Human Capital Approach." *Journal of Economic Literature* (March 1970), pp. 1-26.

Mincer, Jacob. *Schooling, Experience, and Earnings*. New York: Columbia University Press, 1974.

Mincer, Jacob. "Family Migration Decision." Unpublished mimeograph. January 1976.

Mincer, Jacob, and Solomon Polachek. "Family Investments in Human Capital: Earnings of Women." *Journal of Political Economy* (March/April 1974, part II), pp. S76-108.

Mott, Frank L., and Sylvia F. Moore. "The Dynamics of Marital Disruption:

Determinants and Consequences." Paper presented at the Population Association Meetings, St. Louis, Missouri. April 1977.

Nagely, Donna L. "Traditional and Pioneer Working Mothers." *Journal of Vocational Behavior* 1 (October 1971), pp. 331-341.

National Center for Health Statistics. "Final Divorce Statistics, 1975." *Monthly Vital Statistics Report*, vol. 26, no. 2 - supplement 2. Washington, D.C.: Public Health Service, U.S. Department of Health, Education and Welfare, May 19, 1977.

Oaxaca, Ronald. "Male-Female Wage Differentials in Urban Labor Markets." *International Economic Review* (October 1973), pp. 693-709.

Oppenheimer, Valarie Kincaid. "The Sex-Labeling of Jobs." *Industrial Relations* 7 (May 1973), pp. 219-234.

Parsons, Donald O. "Quit Rates Over Time: A Search and Information Approach." *American Economic Review* (June 1973), pp. 390-401.

Plateris, Alexander A. *100 Years of Marriage and Divorce Statistics.* Vital and Health Statistics Series 21, no. 24. Washington, D.C.: Division of Vital Statistics, National Center for Health Statistics, 1973.

Polachek, Solomon. "Occupational Segregation: An Alternative Hypothesis." *Journal of Contemporary Business* 5 (Winter 1976), pp. 1-12.

Pope, Hallowell, and Charles W. Mueller. "The Intergenerational Transmission of Marital Instability." *Journal of Social Issues* 32 (1976), pp. 49-66.

Priebe, John A., Joan Heinkel, and Stanley Greene. *1970 Occupation and Industry Classification Systems in Terms of Their 1960 Occupation and Industry Elements.* U.S. Bureau of the Census Technical Paper no. 26. Washington, D.C.: U.S. Government Printing Office, 1972.

Radner, R., and L.S. Miller. "Economics of Education: Demand and Supply in U.S. Higher Education: A Progress Report." *American Economic Review* 60 (May 1970), pp. 326-334.

Roe, Anne. *The Making of a Scientist.* New York: Dodd, Mead, 1953.

Rosen, Sherwin. "Learning and Experience in the Labor Market." *Journal of Human Resources* (Summer 1972), pp. 326-342.

Ross, Heather, and Isabel Sawhill. *Time of Transition.* Washington, D.C.: The Urban Institute, 1975.

Sandell, Steven H. "The Economics of Family Migration." In *Dual Careers*, vol. IV. Columbus: The Ohio State University, Center for Human Resource Research, December 1975.

Sandell, Steven H. "The Demand for College Quality." Mimeographed. Columbus: The Ohio State University, Center for Human Resource Research, 1977.

Sandell, Steven H., and David Shapiro. "The Theory of Human Capital and the Earnings of Women: A Re-examination of the Evidence." Mimeographed. Columbus: The Ohio State University, Center for Human Resource Research, 1976.

Sandell, Steven H., and David Shapiro. "The Theory of Human Capital and the

Earnings of Women: A Re-examination of the Evidence." *Journal of Human Resources* (Winter 1978).

Schwartz, Aba. "Migration and Life Span Earnings in the United States." Ph.D. dissertation, University of Chicago, 1968.

Shapiro, David. "Specific Human Capital, Job Tenure, and the Earnings of Women." Mimeographed. Columbus: The Ohio State University, 1976.

Shister, Joseph. "Labor Mobility: Some Institutional Aspects." *Industrial Relations Research Association Proceedings of Third Annual Meeting* (1950), pp. 42-59.

Shortlidge, Richard, and Patricia Brito. *How Women Arrange for the Care of Their Children While They Work: A Study of Child Care Arrangements, Costs, and Preferences in 1971.* Columbus: The Ohio State University, Center for Human Resource Research, 1977.

Solmon, Lewis C. "Schooling and Subsequent Success: The Influence of Ability, Background, and Formal Education." In *Does College Matter? Some Evidence on the Impact of Higher Education,* eds. L. Solomon and P. Taubman. New York: Academic Press, 1973.

Suchar, E., W. Van Dusen, and E.G. Jacobson. *Student Expenses at Postsecondary Institutions 1974-75.* New York: College Entrance Examination Board, 1974.

Taubman, Paul, and Terence Wales. "Mental Ability and Higher Educational Attainment in the Twentieth Century." In *Education, Income, and Human Behavior,* ed. F. Thomas Juster. New York: McGraw-Hill, 1975.

Theil, Henri. *Principles of Econometrics.* New York: John Wiley and Sons, 1971.

Treiman, Donald J., and Kermit Terrell. "Women, Work, and Wages—Trends in the Female Occupation Structure." In *Social Indicator Models,* eds. Kenneth C. Land and Seymour Spilerman. New York: Russell Sage Foundation, 1975, pp. 157-199.

U.S. Bureau of the Census, Technical Paper no. 7. *The Current Population Survey—A Report on Methodology.* Washington, D.C.: U.S. Government Printing Office, 1963.

U.S. Bureau of the Census, *Current Population Reports,* Series P-25, no. 352. "Estimates of the Population of the United States by Age, Color, and Sex: July 1, 1966." Washington, D.C.: U.S. Government Printing Office, November 18, 1966.

U.S. Bureau of the Census, Census of Population: 1970. Final Report PC(2)-6A, *Employment Status and Work Experience.* Washington, D.C.: U.S. Government Printing Office.

U.S. Bureau of the Census, Census of the Population: 1970. Subject Report PC(2)-7A, *Occupational Characteristics.* Washington, D.C.: U.S. Government Printing Office, 1973.

U.S. Bureau of the Census. "Number, Timing, and Duration of Marriage: June 1975." *Current Population Reports* 23 (12). Washington, D.C.: U.S. Government Printing Office, June 1975.

U.S. Department of Labor, Bureau of Labor Statistics. *Occupational Outlook Handbook*, 1968. Bulletin 1550. Washington, D.C.: U.S. Government Printing Office, 1968.

U.S. Department of Labor, Bureau of Labor Statistics. *Occupational Outlook Handbook*, 1972-73. Bulletin 1700. Washington, D.C.: U.S. Government Printing Office, 1972.

U.S. Department of Labor, Bureau of Labor Statistics. *Occupational Outlook Handbook*, 1974-75. Bulletin 1785. Washington, D.C.: U.S. Government Printing Office, 1974.

U.S. Department of Labor, Employment and Training Administration. *Employment and Training Report of the President*. Washington, D.C.: U.S. Government Printing Office, 1976.

U.S. Department of Labor, Manpower Administration, Unemployment Insurance Service. *Comparison of State Unemployment Insurance Laws*. Washington, D.C.: U.S. Government Printing Office, 1973.

Wachtel, Paul. "The Returns to Investment in Higher Education: Another View." In *Education, Income, and Human Behavior*, ed. F. Thomas Juster. New York: McGraw-Hill, 1975.

Wadycki, W.J. "Alternative Opportunities and Interstate Migration: Some Additional Results." *Review of Economics and Statistics* 56 (May 1974), pp. 254-257.

Zellner, Harriet. "The Determinants of Occupational Segregation." *Sex, Discrimination, and the Division of Labor*, ed. Cynthia Lloyd. New York: Columbia University Press, 1975, pp. 125-143.

# Index

# About the Authors

**Frank L. Mott** is the Associate Project Director for the National Longitudinal Surveys in the Center for Human Resource Research as well as an adjunct associate professor in the Faculty of Labor and Human Resources at The Ohio State University. He has written extensively on issues related to women in the labor force, concentrating on the relevance of demographic phenomena for interpreting changing social and economic trends in this area.

**Steven H. Sandell** is an assistant professor of economics at The Ohio State University as well as a senior research associate in the Center for Human Resource Research, and has published extensively on various theoretical and policy related aspects of labor and human resources. His areas of interest include geographic mobility, human capital investment, and unemployment analysis, with particular focus on their implications for women in American society.

**David Shapiro** also is an assistant professor of economics at Ohio State as well as a Center senior research associate. His publications include research on human capital investment, the economics of education, and the effects of unionization on wages.

**Carol Jusenius** is an assistant professor in the Department of City and Regional Planning at The Ohio State University, and has published extensively on research and policy issues relating to the status of women in the United States.

**Timothy J. Carr** and **Sylvia F. Moore** are graduate research associates in the Center for Human Resource Research, and **Patricia K. Brito** and **Peter J. Koenig** until recently were associated with the Center.